GAO

Report to the Chairman, Subcommittee on Government Efficiency, Financial Management and Intergovernmental Relations, Committee on Government Reform, House of Representatives

February 2001

INFORMATION SECURITY

Advances and Remaining Challenges to Adoption of Public Key Infrastructure Technology

GAO-01-277

Contents

Abbreviations

ACES   Access Certificates for Electronic Services
API   application programming interface
CA   certification authority
CIO   chief information officer
DMS   Defense Message System
DOD   Department of Defense
DOE   Department of Energy
DTS   Defense Travel System

ECA	external certification authority
FBCA	Federal Bridge Certification Authority
FDIC	Federal Deposit Insurance Corporation
FPKISC	Federal PKI Steering Committee
GITS	Government Information Technology Services
GSA	General Services Administration
GTRI	Georgia Tech Research Institute
IETF	Internet Engineering Task Force
IRS	Internal Revenue Service
IT	information technology
NASA	National Aeronautics and Space Administration
NIST	National Institute of Standards and Technology
OMB	Office of Management and Budget
PEBES	Personal Earnings and Benefit Estimate Statement
PIN	personal identification number
PKI	public key infrastructure
SSA	Social Security Administration
SSL	secure sockets layer

G A O
Accountability * Integrity * Reliability

United States General Accounting Office
Washington, D.C. 20548

February 26, 2001

The Honorable Stephen Horn
Chairman, Subcommittee on Government Efficiency,
    Financial Management and Intergovernmental Relations
Committee on Government Reform
House of Representatives

Dear Mr. Chairman:

This report responds to your request that we review the federal government's public key infrastructure (PKI) strategy and initiatives to assess the issues and challenges the government faces in adopting this new technology. A PKI is a system of hardware, software, policies, and people that, when fully and properly implemented, can provide a suite of information security assurances that are important in protecting sensitive communications and transactions. Specifically, we agreed to assess (1) the progress of the federal government in planning and coordinating federal PKI initiatives and (2) remaining challenges to be overcome before PKI can be put into widespread use. The report recommends that the Director of the Office of Management and Budget take steps to improve the federal government's planning for adoption of PKI technology.

We are sending copies of this report to Representative Dan Burton, Chairman, and Representative Henry A. Waxman, Ranking Minority Member, House Committee on Government Reform; and to Representative Janice D. Schakowsky, Ranking Minority Member of your Subcommittee. We are also sending a copy of this report to the Honorable Mitchell E. Daniels, Director, Office of Management and Budget. This report will also be available on GAO's home page at *http://www.gao.gov.*

If you have any questions concerning this report, please call me at (202) 512-6257 or send e-mail to *mcclured@gao.gov.* Other major contributors included John de Ferrari, Steven Law, John C. Martin, and Jamelyn Smith.

Sincerely yours,

David L. McClure
Director, Information Technology Management Issues

Executive Summary

Purpose

The federal government is increasingly promoting PKI technology for many electronic government applications. A PKI is a system of hardware, software, policies, and people that, when fully and properly implemented, can provide a suite of information security assurances that are important in protecting sensitive communications and transactions. Given the importance of PKI as an enabler of electronic government, GAO agreed to identify (1) the progress of the federal government in planning and coordinating federal PKI initiatives and (2) remaining challenges to be overcome before PKI can be put into widespread use.

Background

Increasingly, federal agencies are using the World Wide Web and other Internet-based applications to provide on-line public access to information and services as well as to improve internal business operations. Congressional interest in the potential benefits of electronic and Internet-based operations has resulted in the passage of laws designed to encourage the deployment of electronic government functions. However, the potential for improvements in service delivery and productivity come with many of the security risks faced by existing systems as well as new risks. In some cases, the sensitive information and communications that may be involved in these activities will require greater security assurances than can be provided by simple security measures, such as requiring passwords to gain access to a system. A PKI and its associated hardware, software, policies, and people can provide these greater assurances. Some electronic government functions, such as the dissemination of public information, probably do not need such rigorous measures. However, many important communications and transactions that involve sensitive personal and financial data cannot safely be conducted through purely electronic means until the critical security features such as those provided by PKI are enabled. The Chief Information Officer (CIO) Council's Federal PKI Steering Committee (FPKISC) and the General Services Administration (GSA) have been the chief promoters of PKI technology in the federal government. Regarding overall direction on governmentwide information resources and technology management, the Office of Management and Budget (OMB) is responsible for overseeing the efficiency and effectiveness of interagency information technology initiatives and developing and overseeing implementation of privacy and security policies, standards, and guidelines.

Results in Brief

The Federal PKI Steering Committee, in conjunction with GSA, has made progress in promoting the adoption of PKI by individual agencies and in laying the groundwork for the future development of a broader governmentwide PKI. The committee has developed a mechanism, called the Federal Bridge Certification Authority (FBCA), to connect disparate agency PKI applications into a broader system. In addition, GSA is sponsoring a program designed to develop and provide some of the elements of an "off the shelf" PKI to individual agencies to promote wider adoption of the technology. Several agencies—including the Department of Defense (DOD), the Department of Energy (DOE), the Federal Deposit Insurance Corporation (FDIC), the National Aeronautics and Space Administration (NASA), and the U.S. Patent and Trademark Office—have already implemented or are in the process of implementing PKI systems.

Although progress has been made in seeding PKI technology throughout the government, designing and implementing large-scale systems that use PKI technology remains a daunting task. Full-featured PKI implementations—those that offer all of the security assurances needed for sensitive communications and transactions—are not yet commonplace in either the government or the private sector, and a number of substantial challenges must be overcome before the technology can be widely and effectively deployed.

- First, in order to develop an interoperable[1] governmentwide system, agency PKIs will have to work seamlessly with each other, yet current PKI products and implementations suffer from interoperability problems.
- Second, because full-featured PKIs are rare, and those that exist are in the early stages of implementation and use, it is not yet known how well this technology will truly scale and interoperate as its use grows.
- Third, adoption of the technology may be impeded by the high cost associated with building a PKI and enabling software applications to use it. These costs can easily add up to millions of dollars.
- Fourth, an effective PKI—at any level within the government—will require well-defined policies and procedures for ensuring that an appropriate level of security is maintained on an ongoing basis. Establishing such policies will require resolution of a number of

---

[1]Interoperability is the ability of two or more systems or components to exchange information and to use the information that has been exchanged.

sensitive issues in areas such as privacy protection, encryption key recovery, and how employees will be expected to identify themselves and secure their electronic keys.

- Finally, as with any security technology, the success of a PKI implementation will depend on how well people interact with the system and how well the system is implemented. Thus, federal agencies will be faced with the challenge of training and involving both users and system administrators in the adoption of a technology that many find complex and difficult to understand.

A logical way to address the uncertainties and risks involved in adopting PKI technology in the government is to establish and enforce a governmentwide management framework to guide the development and deployment of PKIs by federal agencies. Although the FPKISC has made efforts at a grass-roots level to facilitate the eventual development of a governmentwide PKI, it does not have the authority to define or require adherence to a governmentwide management framework. Without such a framework, agencies risk building and buying systems that are not interoperable and thus may require costly, complex solutions to interact with a governmentwide PKI.

Principal Findings

The Federal Government Has Made Progress in Planning and Coordinating PKI Initiatives

To further the development and deployment of secure electronic government, a number of public key technology initiatives have begun at the governmentwide level as well as at individual agencies. FPKISC has been working to broaden awareness of the benefits of PKI technology and to promote coordination of PKI activities throughout the government. Most notable is the FBCA, connecting agency PKI applications. A prototype version has been constructed, and some of its key features have been successfully tested. For example, the demonstration successfully validated signature certifications through complex chains of certification authorities, including some that were up to seven certification authorities in length. Committee officials are confident that an operational version of the bridge certification authority will function as planned. A production version is under construction and is expected to be available for operation in the second quarter of fiscal year 2001. A managing body, the Federal PKI Policy Authority, has recently been established to oversee and coordinate agency involvement in the bridge certification authority.

GSA's program to provide free to agencies elements of an "off the shelf" PKI for government transactions made directly with the general public—called Access Certificates for Electronic Services (ACES)—has been successful in jump-starting the effort. The Social Security Administration and the Federal Emergency Management Administration are two agencies that are planning to make use of ACES to build PKI technology into some of their applications. Several other agencies—including DOD, DOE, FDIC, NASA, and the U.S. Patent and Trademark Office—have already implemented or are in the process of implementing PKI projects independently of the ACES program.

Full PKI Implementation Faces Many Formidable Challenges

Despite recent progress, designing and implementing systems fully able to utilize PKI technology within the government remains a serious challenge. Several significant issues must be addressed before the technology can be widely and effectively deployed, including the following.

- *Interoperability.* In order to develop an interconnected governmentwide system, agency PKIs will have to work seamlessly with each other, yet current products and implementations suffer from significant interoperability problems, largely because PKI is not yet well-established and standards are not yet complete. Several different strategies will be needed to solve this problem, including further refining existing standards, adopting standard high-level interfaces—commonly referred to as application programming interfaces[2]—and developing mechanisms such as the FBCA, which acts as a bridge across disparate agency systems. However, none of these solutions is easy or can be adopted quickly.
- *Operational experience.* Government PKI implementations that offer the full range of security assurances that may be needed for sensitive communications and transactions currently exist only in limited pilot projects or within relatively small, well-defined communities. For example, the Patent and Trademark Office's Electronic Patent Application Filing System serves a relatively small population of patent attorneys. Because no full-featured PKI has yet been implemented on a truly broad scale—such as a major federal agency—many questions

---

[2]An application programming interface is the point of interaction between the application software and the application platform (i.e., operating system), across which all services are provided.

remain about whether the products, which are currently available to implement PKI, can meet the demands of widespread use.

- *Affordability.* Although PKI's security features are critical to enabling many important electronic government transactions and can be viewed as an investment in providing security services for a wide range of applications, adoption of PKI technology may be impeded by the high cost associated with building a PKI and enabling software applications to use it. Systems must be set up to carry out the technical functions of a PKI, including positively identifying internal and external users, generating keys, issuing them digital certificates, and managing the exchange and verification of certificates. In addition, existing software applications, electronic directories, and other legacy systems must be modified so they can interact with the PKI. Further, outside vendors that conduct electronic business with an agency will likely incur costs and disruptions in making their own systems compatible. As a result, the total costs associated with building a PKI and enabling applications to use it can easily add up to millions of dollars.

- *Well-defined and enforced policies and procedures.* An effective PKI—at any level within the government—will require a well-defined set of policies and procedures for ensuring that the security of the system is maintained on an ongoing basis. Establishing and enforcing these policies and procedures will require resolution of a range of sensitive issues. For example, because the digital certificates that PKI systems produce and application programs use could also serve as a way to track individuals as they conduct business throughout the federal government, measures will have to be put in place to protect users' privacy. Further, procedures will have to be developed stipulating how employees will be expected to identify themselves and secure their electronic keys and what actions will be taken when keys are lost or destroyed. Developing, implementing, and enforcing a complete set of policies and procedures is likely to require a substantial effort on the part of each federal agency.

- *Trained personnel.* As with any security technology, the success of a PKI implementation will depend on how well people interact with the system and how well the system is implemented. However, PKI technology in particular is complex and difficult for many people to grasp. Even a well-designed and well-implemented PKI will lose its effectiveness if users do not properly safeguard their keys and do not understand the inherent vulnerabilities associated with Web browsers, such as improperly accepting unverified digital certificates.

To date, federal agencies have not been directed by any governmentwide standards for developing and managing PKIs. Early agency PKI pilot projects have been focused on narrow communities of interest and have not addressed larger compatibility problems. A management framework could help agencies address the many challenges involved in implementing PKI technology. Several key guidance areas essential to a federal PKI management framework are currently not well defined, including (1) a program plan identifying roles and responsibilities at the governmentwide and agency levels as well as general time frames and resources to develop, deploy, and maintain a federal PKI, (2) policy standards to reduce implementation issues and efforts spent by federal agencies to develop unique PKI solutions, and (3) technical standards—a federal PKI architecture—that can guide the development and integration of agency PKIs. In order to provide more and better electronic services, the government needs a management framework, including a federal PKI architecture that specifies standard protocols and high-level application programming interfaces (API) to provide better guidance and promote interoperability among agencies' PKIs.

Recommendations for Executive Action

Given OMB's statutory responsibility to develop and oversee policies, principles, standards, and guidelines used by agencies for ensuring the security of federal information systems, we recommend that the Director, OMB establish a governmentwide framework to provide agencies with direction for implementing PKIs. In constructing this framework OMB needs to develop federal PKI policy guidance and ensure (1) the development and periodic review of technical guidance, (2) the preparation of a federal PKI program plan, and (3) that agencies are adhering to federal PKI policy and technical guidance. In implementing these recommendations, OMB should work with other key federal organizations, especially the CIO Council, FPKISC, and National Institute of Standards and Technology, to ensure broad acceptance within the federal government. Details of our recommendations are provided in the report.

Agency Comments and Our Evaluation

We received comments on a draft of this report from the Branch Chief for Information Policy, Office of Information and Regulatory Affairs, OMB; Deputy Assistant Secretary (Information Systems) and Chief Information Officer, Department of the Treasury; Associate Administrator, Office of Governmentwide Policy, GSA; Deputy Assistant Secretary of Defense (Security and Information Operations), DOD; and the Chairman of the

FPKISC. All of the agency officials who reviewed the draft agreed with the overall content of the report. Officials from OMB and GSA were concerned that our recommendations language would lead OMB to adopt an overly prescriptive "how to" role in federal PKI implementation. In response to this concern, we have clarified the language outlining our recommendations regarding OMB's role. We are recommending that OMB establish a general PKI management framework to better facilitate the use of PKI technology, ensure that agency PKI applications meet consistent levels of security, and reduce the overall risk to the government of developing disparate PKI implementations. In addition, each agency provided technical comments, which have been addressed where appropriate in the final report. Letters from GSA and Treasury are reprinted in appendixes III and IV. Specific issues raised by reviewing agencies, along with our responses, are discussed in chapter 3.

Chapter 1

Background

Increasingly, federal agencies are using the World Wide Web and other Internet-based applications to provide on-line public access to information and services as well as to improve internal business operations. In some cases, the sensitive information and communications that may be involved in these activities will require a range of security assurances. Fully and properly implemented, a PKI is a system of hardware, software, policies, and people that can provide these assurances. Some electronic government functions, such as the dissemination of public information, probably do not need such rigorous measures. However, many important communications and transactions that involve sensitive personal and financial data cannot safely be conducted through purely electronic means until all of the critical security features provided by PKI are enabled.

The Adoption of Electronic Government May Be Slowed by Security Concerns

Electronic government—made possible by widespread Internet access and interconnected systems—has the potential to transform how the federal government operates. Electronic government is being pursued to facilitate interaction of citizens and businesses with their government and improve the efficiency and effectiveness of government through the application of information technology (IT) resources. Electronic government can include activities such as information collection and dissemination, funds and benefits transfers, filings and applications, revenue collection, and procurement of goods and services. For example, the Internal Revenue Service (IRS), the Department of Education, and the Social Security Administration (SSA) have applied electronic government techniques to improve service delivery to taxpayers, students, and senior citizens, respectively. Agencies such as DOD, NASA, and GSA have implemented on-line procurement operations for several years.[1]

Congressional interest in the potential benefits of electronic and Internet-based operations has resulted in laws designed to encourage the deployment of electronic government functions. For example, the Clinger-Cohen Act of 1996 requires GSA to provide governmentwide on-line access to information about products and services available under the multiple award schedules program. The National Defense Authorization Act for

---

[1]GAO products discussing electronic government issues include *Electronic Government: Government Paperwork Elimination Act Presents Challenges for Agencies* (GAO/AIMD-00-282, September 15, 2000) and *Electronic Government: Federal Initiatives Are Evolving Rapidly But They Face Significant Challenges* (GAO/T-AIMD/GGD-00-179, May 22, 2000).

Fiscal Year 1999 required DOD to establish a single, Defense-wide electronic mall system for ordering supplies and materials. More broadly, the Government Paperwork Elimination Act of 1998[2] set a deadline of October 2003 for agencies to develop capabilities to permit, where practicable, electronic maintenance, submission, or disclosure of information, including the use of electronic signatures. Further, the Electronic Signatures in Global and National Commerce Act[3] provides, with certain exceptions, a signature or contract may not be denied legal effect solely because it is in electronic form.

The potential for improvements in service delivery and productivity offered by electronic government also involves threats, risks, and liabilities. Although the risks to electronic systems and the traditional systems they are designed to replace may be similar, the levels of risk may be vastly different. For example, electronic transactions lack the physical context of traditional transactions and thus involve increased risk. A paper record of a transaction can undergo forensic chemical analysis to determine whether it has been altered; however, electronic records in many systems can be altered without detection. Further, physical access is needed before a paper record can be tampered with, and such access is inherently limited. On the other hand, with the global reach of the Internet, electronic misuse and tampering can occur more quickly and with far greater impact. Finally, human participation is required on both sides of a paper-based transaction, providing the opportunity for immediate human inspection and verification of the transaction. In contrast, electronic systems may readily process transactions that would be immediately suspicious to a human observer. Unless special security features are properly implemented, electronic transactions are much more susceptible to fraud and abuse than traditional paper-based transactions.

In addition, electronic government transactions will have to take place in an environment of persistent information security weaknesses. Known computer and network vulnerabilities—as well as the automated attack tools needed to exploit them—are increasingly being made publicly available, for example, by being posted on the Internet. This offers potential attackers having only limited technical skill and knowledge the

---

[2]Government Paperwork Elimination Act, Public Law 105-277, October 21, 1998.

[3]Electronic Signatures in Global and National Commerce Act, Public Law 106-229, June 30, 2000.

opportunity to cause a great deal of damage. Business risks such as fraud, theft, and destruction of assets—along with legal issues such as liability and the loss of reputation—are exacerbated by the openness of the Internet. Stories in the press of hacker attacks, Web page defacements, and credit card information posted on electronic bulletin boards have led to legitimate concerns about conducting "real" business over the Internet. Recent surveys indicate that security and privacy are top concerns among world Internet users.[4] These concerns are not unjustified. In recent years we have consistently found security weaknesses at many federal agencies, some of which could place sensitive tax, medical, and other personal records at risk of unauthorized disclosure.[5]

Sensitive Transactions Face Special Challenges

In recent years, valuable information about government services and activities has been increasingly available over the Internet. However, expectations are that electronic government will include much more than just the electronic distribution of information; it will also include the application for and delivery of government services on-line. Many such services involve sensitive personal information, which will need to be exchanged electronically. Sensitive information and transactions may need greater security assurances.

SSA's experience in attempting to make individuals' Personal Earnings and Benefit Estimate Statements (PEBES) available on-line showed that extra safeguards may be needed when sensitive personal information is at risk of improper disclosure. In March 1997, SSA first made PEBES information available over the Internet. PEBES provides individuals with detailed information on their earnings by year, Social Security taxes paid, and an estimate of future benefits. The statements had been available in hard copy by mail in response to written requests for about 10 years. To protect the new on-line program, SSA had taken several measures that officials believed would adequately safeguard requesters' privacy, the system itself, and the data it contained. However, just 1 month after the on-line program's

---

[4]See *Assessing E-Government: The Internet, Democracy, and Service Delivery by State and Federal Governments*, Darrell M. West, Brown University, September 2000 and *E-Government: The Next American Revolution*, Hart-Teeter for the Council for Excellence in Government, September 2000.

[5]*Federal Information Security: Actions Needed to Address Widespread Weaknesses* (GAO/T/AIMD-00-135, March 29, 2000) and *Information Security: Serious and Widespread Weaknesses Persist at Federal Agencies* (GAO/AIMD-00-295, September 6, 2000).

implementation, concerns over the adequacy of the privacy safeguards had sparked such public outcry that the Acting Commissioner of SSA was forced to suspend it, although SSA reported that it had not received any allegations of individuals fraudulently accessing the system. Concerns were raised that potential wrongdoers could obtain this information surreptitiously and use it to gain access electronically to an individual's private earnings and benefits information.[6] Others were concerned that wrongdoers could use this service to validate identifying information about an individual that they had obtained from other sources. While citizens can still request PEBES information on-line, the statements are again mailed out in hard copy, taking up to 4 weeks for receipt.

Sensitive Transactions Will Likely Need the Full Range of Security Assurances Offered by PKI

Transactions involving sensitive information, such as PEBES statements, are likely to require greater security assurances than can be had through simple security measures, such as requiring passwords to gain access to a system. For any given application, federal agencies are responsible for determining the type of on-line transactions to be conducted over the Internet and the security requirements needed to protect those transactions.[7] Examples of sensitive transactions include the filing of income tax forms with the IRS, applications for student financial aid with the Department of Education, and applications for loans with the Small Business Administration. Many federal information security experts believe that sensitive government transactions such as these cannot be safely conducted through purely electronic means until a full range of critical security features are enabled. According to the National Institute of Standards and Technology (NIST), individuals or entities interacting with federal agencies electronically where there is a need for a secure transaction should have four kinds of security assurances.[8]

- *Identification and authentication* is the assurance that the information sender and the recipient will both be identified uniquely so that both

---

[6]See *Social Security Administration: Internet Access to Personal Earnings and Benefits Information* (GAO/T-AIMD/HEHS-97-123, May 6, 1997).

[7]OMB Memorandum M-00-10, *OMB Procedures and Guidance on Implementing the Government Paperwork Elimination Act*, April 25, 2000.

[8]*Federal Agency Use of Public Key Technology for Digital Signatures and Authentication* (NIST Special Publication 800-25, September 2000).

parties know where the information is coming from and where it is going.

- *Confidentiality*, or privacy, is the assurance that the information will be protected from unauthorized access.
- *Data integrity* is the assurance that data have not been accidentally or deliberately altered.
- *Nonrepudiation* provides proof of the integrity and origin of data that can be verified by a third party. Nonrepudiation services may provide important legal evidence in the event of a dispute.

Most security techniques in common use today provide only a subset of these security features. For example, traditional user identification and passwords/personal identification numbers (PIN) only provide for user authentication. By entering a user name and then a password or PIN when beginning a transaction, a user "proves" his or her identity to the system, because only the legitimate user should know the correct password/PIN. The system can then determine what types of transactions that user is authorized to make.[9]

However, for many sensitive government transactions, this level of security is not enough to satisfy the needs of either the end user or the government agency involved. Users may also want assurance that they are indeed connected to the particular agency they wish to do business with (authentication of the recipient of the data as well as the sender). Furthermore, both parties to the potential transaction may want assurance that the amount and other details of the transaction will be kept private (confidentiality) and will not be altered, either accidentally or otherwise, as the transaction is being processed (data integrity). And finally, they may want some kind of irrefutable electronic "receipt" to prove that the transaction was actually submitted by the end user and received by the government (nonrepudiation).

Fully and properly implemented, PKI can provide these types of assurances so that sensitive transactions can be adequately secured. Given that passwords and PINs are inadequate in this situation, PKI technology

---

[9]Although passwords and PINs are designed to provide this safeguard, in practice we have found that the controls over these systems are often compromised. For a recent example, see *Financial Management Service: Significant Weaknesses in Computer Controls* (GAO/AIMD-00-305, September 26, 2000).

represents one possible solution. The various technical features of PKI that can provide security assurances are discussed further in this chapter.

Commonly available commercial Web browsers (such as Microsoft's Internet Explorer and America Online's Netscape Communicator) make use of only some of the technical features of PKI to provide security for Web-enabled transactions. They invoke a standardized information exchange protocol known as secure sockets layer (SSL), which uses PKI-like features to provide a limited form of authentication between a user application, such as a Web browser, and a server. In addition, many Web-based merchants use SSL to provide confidentiality for customer purchase information as it traverses the Internet. However, the full range of security assurances that may be needed for sensitive transactions is not available through SSL, unless the user's software is specially configured or modified. As it is commonly used, SSL does not provide full authentication of both sender and recipient, nor does it provide for nonrepudiation of a transaction. Thus it is not an answer to all of the government's needs in securing sensitive electronic transactions. (See appendix I for a discussion of the limitations of SSL.) On the other hand, an effective full-featured PKI is a practical option available to satisfactorily address all of the security assurances that may be needed for these transactions. Again, the entity developing the PKI is responsible for determining the security requirements needed to conduct and protect on-line transactions.

OMB is responsible for providing direction on governmentwide information resources and technology management and overseeing agency activities in these areas. These responsibilities include assessing the efficiency and effectiveness of interagency IT initiatives. OMB is also responsible for developing and overseeing implementation of privacy and security policies, principles, standards, and guidelines. OMB has identified various categories of transactions that could require the security assurances provided by a PKI.[10]

- *Transactions involving the transfer of funds.* Examples include Department of Veterans Affairs and SSA claims and benefits.
- *Transactions in which parties commit to actions or contracts that may give rise to financial or legal liability.* Examples include student loans and procurement contracts.

---

[10]OMB Memorandum M-00-10, *OMB Procedures and Guidance on Implementing the Government Paperwork Elimination Act*, April 25, 2000, pages 19-20.

- *Transactions involving information protected under the Privacy Act or other agency-specific statutes, or information with national security sensitivity, obliging that access to the information be restricted.* Examples include applications for passports and communications within DOD, the Department of State, and the Nuclear Regulatory Commission.
- *Transactions in which the party is fulfilling a legal responsibility that, if not performed, creates a legal liability.* Examples include selective service registration, environmental reporting to the Environmental Protection Agency, and regulatory filings with the Securities and Exchange Commission.

According to OMB guidance, not all transactions that fall into these categories will necessarily need the full range of PKI security services. Agencies will need to conduct risk assessments of systems to determine the level of protection most appropriate for each. The CIO Council's Federal PKI Steering Committee (FPKISC) is the federal government's focal point for adoption of PKI technology. Through NIST, the committee can provide technical assistance to agencies considering implementing PKI. GSA has also been a promoter of PKI technology for the federal government through its Access Certificates for Electronic Services (ACES) program.

PKI Uses Advanced Cryptographic Techniques to Provide Its Security Assurances

The basis of PKI's security assurances is a sophisticated cryptographic technique known as public key cryptography. PKIs use cryptographic techniques to generate and manage electronic "certificates," which link an individual or entity to a given public key. These certificates are then used to verify digital signatures (providing authentication and data integrity) and facilitate data encryption (providing confidentiality). A properly designed and implemented PKI can also be used to ensure that a given digital signature is still properly linked to the individual or entity associated with it (providing nonrepudiation).

Cryptography is the transformation of ordinary data (commonly referred to as "plaintext") into a code form (ciphertext) and back into plaintext using a special value known as a key and a mathematical process called an algorithm. Cryptography can be used on data to (1) hide their information content, (2) prevent their undetected modification, and/or (3) prevent their unauthorized use. A basic premise in cryptography is that good systems depend only on the secrecy of the key used to perform the operations rather than any attempt to keep the algorithm secret. The algorithms used to perform most cryptographic operations over the Internet are well known; however, because the keys used by these algorithms are kept secret, the process is considered secure.

Cryptographic techniques can be divided into two basic types: secret key and public key cryptography. Properly implemented cryptographic systems can provide assurance regarding the origin, integrity, and confidentiality of the information that has been exchanged, and provide a method by which the authenticity of the document can be confirmed.

Secret Key Cryptography Has Limitations When Used for Large Groups of People With No Preexisting Relationship

Traditionally, the techniques of secret key cryptography have been used primarily to provide confidentiality. In secret key cryptography (also called symmetric key cryptography), one key is used to perform both the encryption and decryption functions. (See figure 1.) The encrypted message can be freely sent from one location to another through an insecure medium, such as the Internet or a telephone link. As the name implies, secret key cryptography relies on both parties keeping the key secret. If this key is compromised, the security offered by the encryption process is eliminated.

Figure 1: Secret Key Cryptography

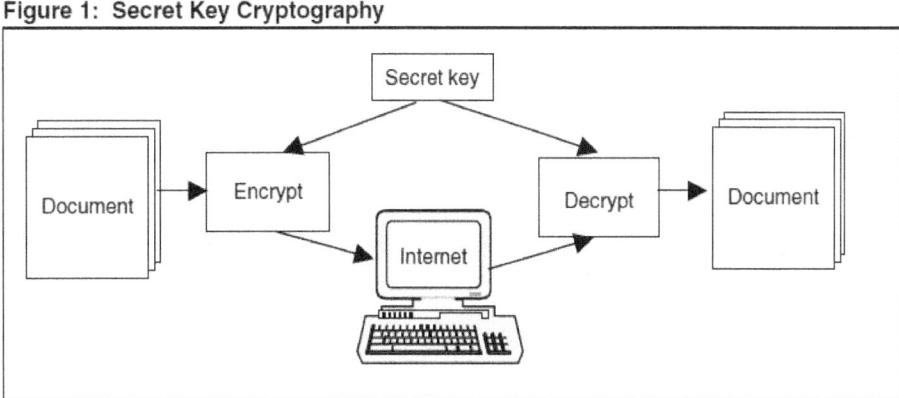

Source: Department of Defense.

Secret key cryptography has significant limitations that can make it impractical as a stand-alone solution for securing electronic transactions, especially among large communities of users that may have no preestablished relationships. The most significant limitation is that some means must be devised to securely distribute and manage the keys that are at the heart of the system, commonly referred to as key management. When many transacting parties are involved, this results in immense logistical problems and delays. Furthermore, in order to minimize the damage that could be caused by a compromised key, the keys may need to be short-lived and therefore frequently changed, adding to the logistical complexity.

Public Key Cryptography Addresses Many of These Limitations

In contrast, public key cryptography (commonly referred to as asymmetric cryptography) uses two different keys—a public key and a private key. The two keys are generated by hardware such as a smart card, software on the user's computer, or provided to the user by a trusted entity. The user keeps one of the keys secret, and the other is made publicly available to other users. The security of the arrangement is based on the fact that knowing the public key does not allow one to know the private key. The two keys are mathematically related so that given the public key, it is computationally infeasible to derive the private key because of the large values used. Key lengths typically range from 512[11] to 1,024 bits,[12] but are likely to grow longer with time.

Suppose a fictional character named Bob has generated his two keys and that he wants other people (or computers) to be able to send encrypted information to him. Bob makes his public key easily accessible by adding it to an on-line database in a manner that irrefutably links the key to his identity. People wishing to send encrypted information to Bob then retrieve his public key and use it to encrypt the information for him.[13] Bob is the only one who can read the information because only his private key is capable of decrypting the message. Of course, Bob must keep his private key well hidden or others will also be able to decrypt information intended for him. In this example, fictional character Alice would encrypt her message to Bob with Bob's freely disclosed public key, which she obtained from an on-line directory of public keys. Bob, in turn, would use his unique private key to decrypt the message. In this way, the confidentially of the message is ensured, as Alice knows that only Bob has the appropriate key

---

[11]Although there are implementations that generate 512-bits keys for digital signatures, those keys do not provide adequate long-term security. Therefore, keys for digital signatures that will be used for long periods of time should be at least 1,024-bits long.

[12]*Digital Signature Standard (DSS)* (NIST Federal Information Processing Standards Publication 186-2, January 27, 2000).

[13]Most public key cryptographic methods can be used for both encryption and digital signatures. However, certain public key methods, most notably the Digital Signature Algorithm, cannot be used for encryption, but only for digital signatures.

to decrypt and read the message. Figure 2 illustrates the basic process of public key cryptography.

Figure 2: Public Key Cryptography

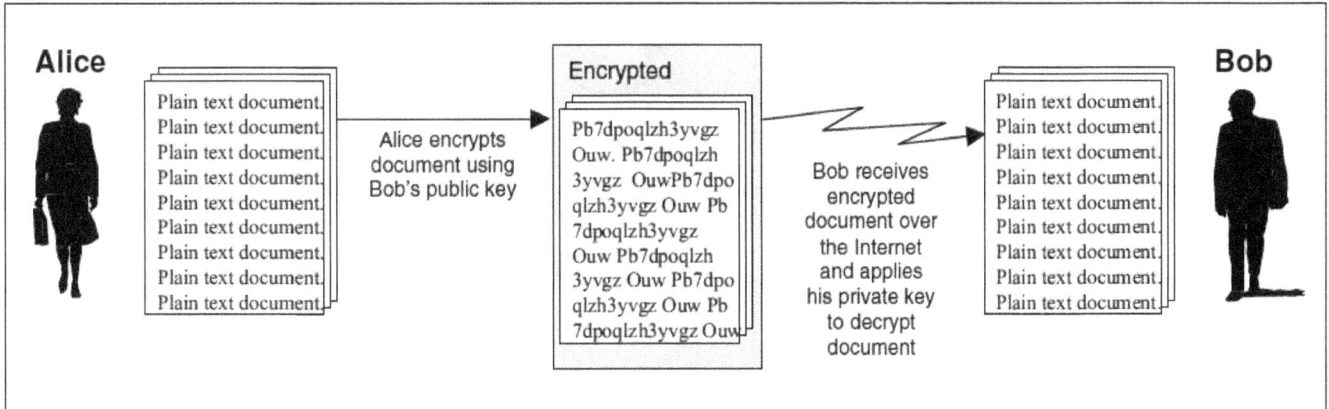

Source: Department of Defense.

Public key cryptography can address many of the limitations of secret key cryptography regarding key management. There is no need to establish a secure channel or physical delivery services to distribute keys. However, public key cryptography has its own challenges involving the methods of ensuring that the links between the users and their public keys are initially valid and are constantly maintained, as will be subsequently discussed.

Combining Secret and Public Key Cryptography Provides Added Benefits

As just described, a sender can provide confidentiality for a message by encrypting it with the recipient's publicly available encryption key using some public key algorithms. However, for large messages, this is computationally time-consuming and could make the whole process unreasonably slow. To solve these problems, it can be better to combine secret and public key cryptography to provide more efficient and effective means by which a sender can encrypt a document so that only the intended recipient can decrypt it. In this case, Alice would generate a one-time secret encryption key (called a "session key") and use it to encrypt the body of her message. Alice would then take Bob's public key, encrypt the one-time session key with that public key, and send him the encrypted session key plus the encrypted document. Bob, in turn, would apply his private key to decrypt the secret session key, then use that session key to decrypt the document itself. A diagram of this process is shown in figure 3.[14]

Figure 3: Combination of Secret and Public Key Cryptography to Encrypt Large Files

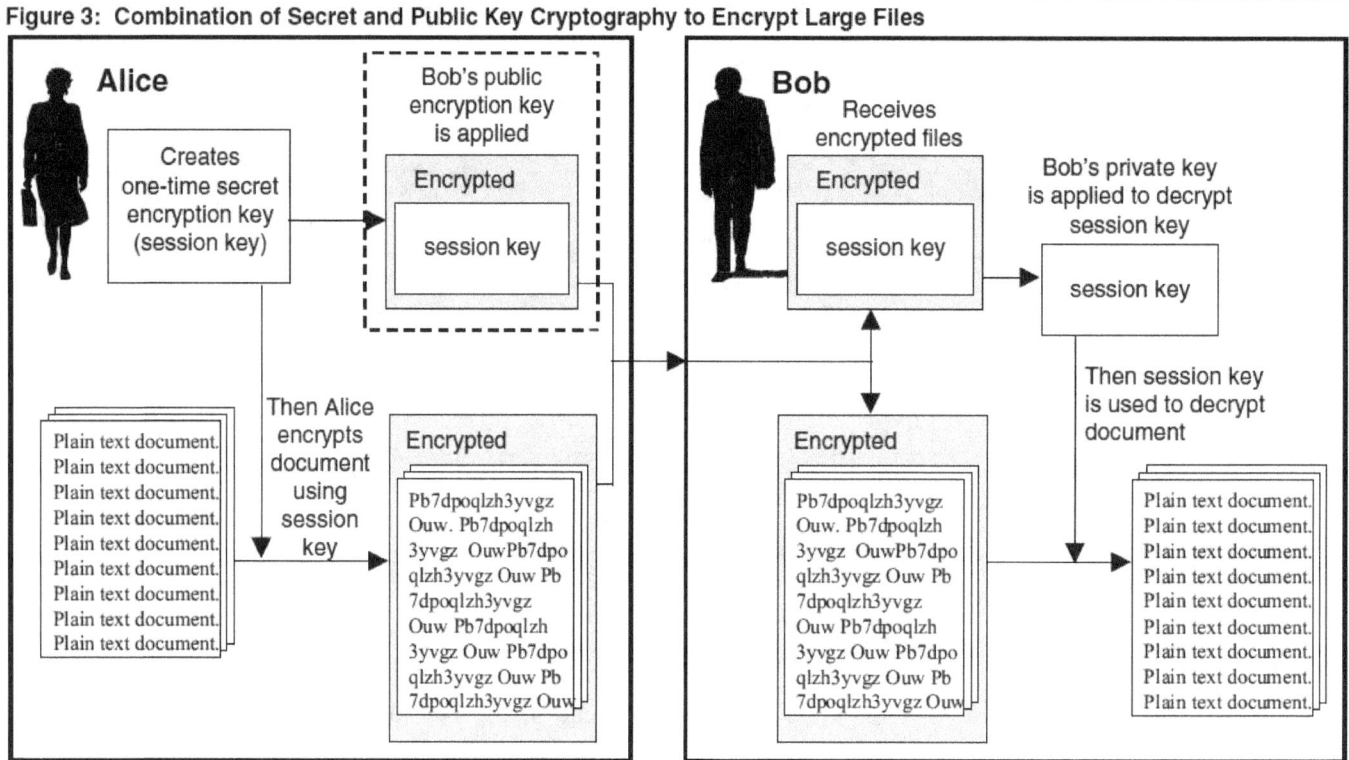

Digital Signatures Are Based on Public Key Cryptography

Public key cryptography can also be used to create a digital signature for a message or transaction, thereby providing authentication, data integrity, and nonrepudiation. For example, if Bob wishes to digitally sign an electronic document, he can use his private key to encrypt it. His public key is freely available, so anyone with access to his public key can decrypt the document. Although this seems backward, since anyone can read what is encrypted, the fact that Bob's private key is held only by Bob provides the basis for Bob's digital signature. If Alice can successfully decrypt the document using Bob's public key, then she knows that the message came

---

[14]Most public key cryptographic methods can be used to combine secret and public keys for encryption. However, as discussed in footnote 13, certain public key methods, most notably the Digital Signature Algorithm, do not support this process.

from Bob, since only he has access to the corresponding private key. Of course, this assumes that (1) Bob has sole control over his private signing key and (2) Alice is sure that the public key used to validate Bob's messages really belongs to Bob.

Digital signature systems use a two-step process, as shown in figure 4. As noted, public key cryptography is not used for encrypting large amounts of data for performance reasons. Therefore, a means is needed to reduce the amount of data that needs to be encrypted. This is accomplished by using a hash algorithm that condenses the data into a message digest. The message digest is encrypted using Bob's private signing key to create a digital signature. Because the message digest will be different for each signature, each signature will also be unique and, using a good hash algorithm, it is computationally infeasible to find another message that will generate the same message digest.

Figure 4: Creating a Digital Signature

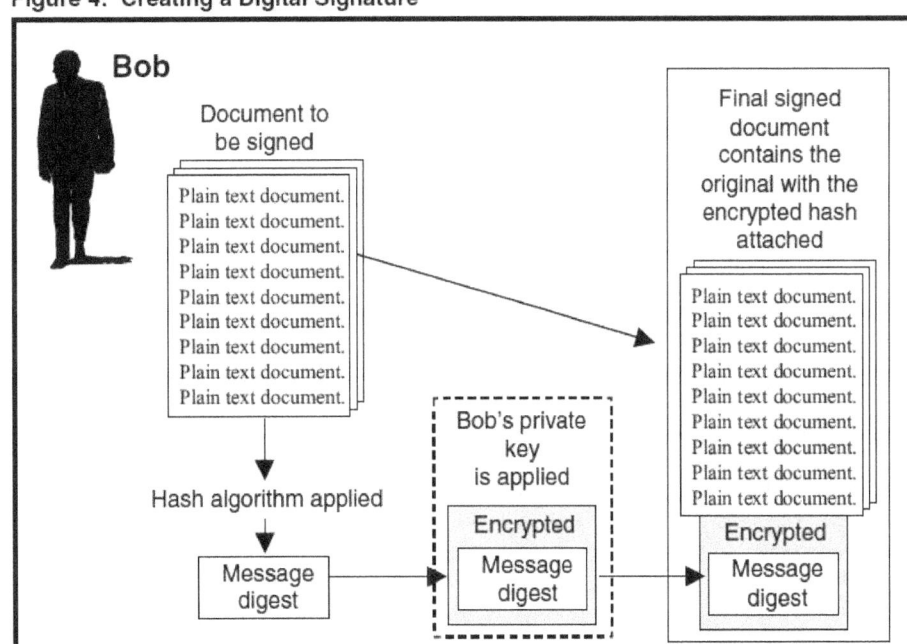

Source: National Institute of Standards and Technology.

Alice (or anyone wishing to verify the document) can compute the message digest of the document and decrypt the signature using Bob's public key, as shown in figure 5. Assuming that the message digests match, Alice then has three kinds of security assurance. First, that Bob actually signed the document (authentication). Second, the digital signature ensures that Bob in fact sent the message (nonrepudiation). And third, since the message digest would have changed if anything in the message had been modified, Alice knows that no one tampered with the contents of the document after Bob signed it (data integrity). Again, this assumes that (1) Bob has sole control over his private signing key and (2) Alice is sure that the public key used to validate Bob's messages really belongs to Bob.

Figure 5: Verifying a Digital Signature

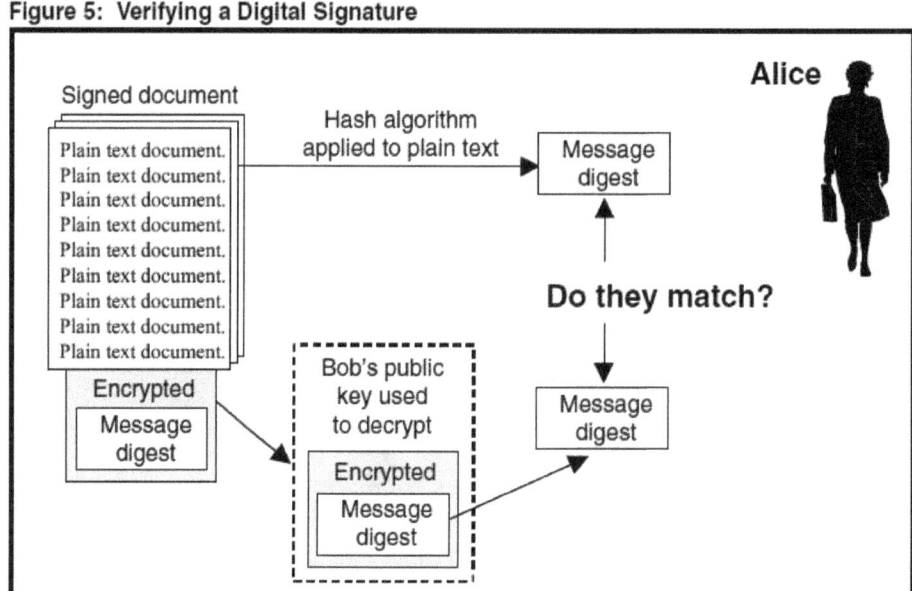

Source: National Institute of Standards and Technology.

Two Sets of Key Pairs are Needed to Support Encryption and Digital Signatures

Within an organizational setting, the security system needs to generate separate key pairs for encryption and for digital signatures. A copy of the user's private encryption key should normally be copied to a safe backup location in case the organization has a need to gain access to encrypted data in situations in which the user's original private encryption key is inaccessible. For example, the organization would have an interest in decrypting data should the private key be destroyed or lost or if the user were fired, incapacitated, or deceased. However, copies should never be made of the private keys used for digital signatures and nonrepudiation, as they could fall into the wrong hands and be used to forge the owner's signatures. In the event that a user loses, breaks, or destroys his private signature key, or forgets how to access it, a new signing key pair can be generated for use from that point forward with minimal impact. Although any subsequent documents signed with the new private signature key must be verified with the new public signature key, previously signed documents can still be verified with the user's old public signature key.

Digital Certificates and Certification Authorities Link Public Keys With Specific Users to Convey Trust

In a small community where everyone knows everyone else, users can individually give their public keys to the people with whom they wish to deal. In a large-scale implementation, where it is necessary for individuals or entities that may not know each other to conduct transactions, it is impractical and unrealistic to expect that each user will have previously established relationships with all of the other potential users in order to obtain their public keys. One way around this problem is for all PKI users and relying entities to mutually agree to trust a third party who is known to everyone. The basic technical components for achieving third-party trust include (1) digital certificates, which link an individual to his or her public key, (2) certification authorities, which create these certificates and vouch for their validity to the entities relying on the PKI, (3) registration authorities, which are in charge of verifying user identities so that the appropriate key pairs and digital certificates can be created, and (4) certification paths, which are used for recognizing and trusting digital certificates issued by other PKIs in order to create larger, connected networks of trust. A set of written policies establishes the security assurances that an organization needs to achieve and the practices and procedures that will be followed to achieve and maintain those assurances. Figure 6 shows the various components of a PKI, each of which will be discussed in more detail.

Figure 6: Basic Components of a PKI

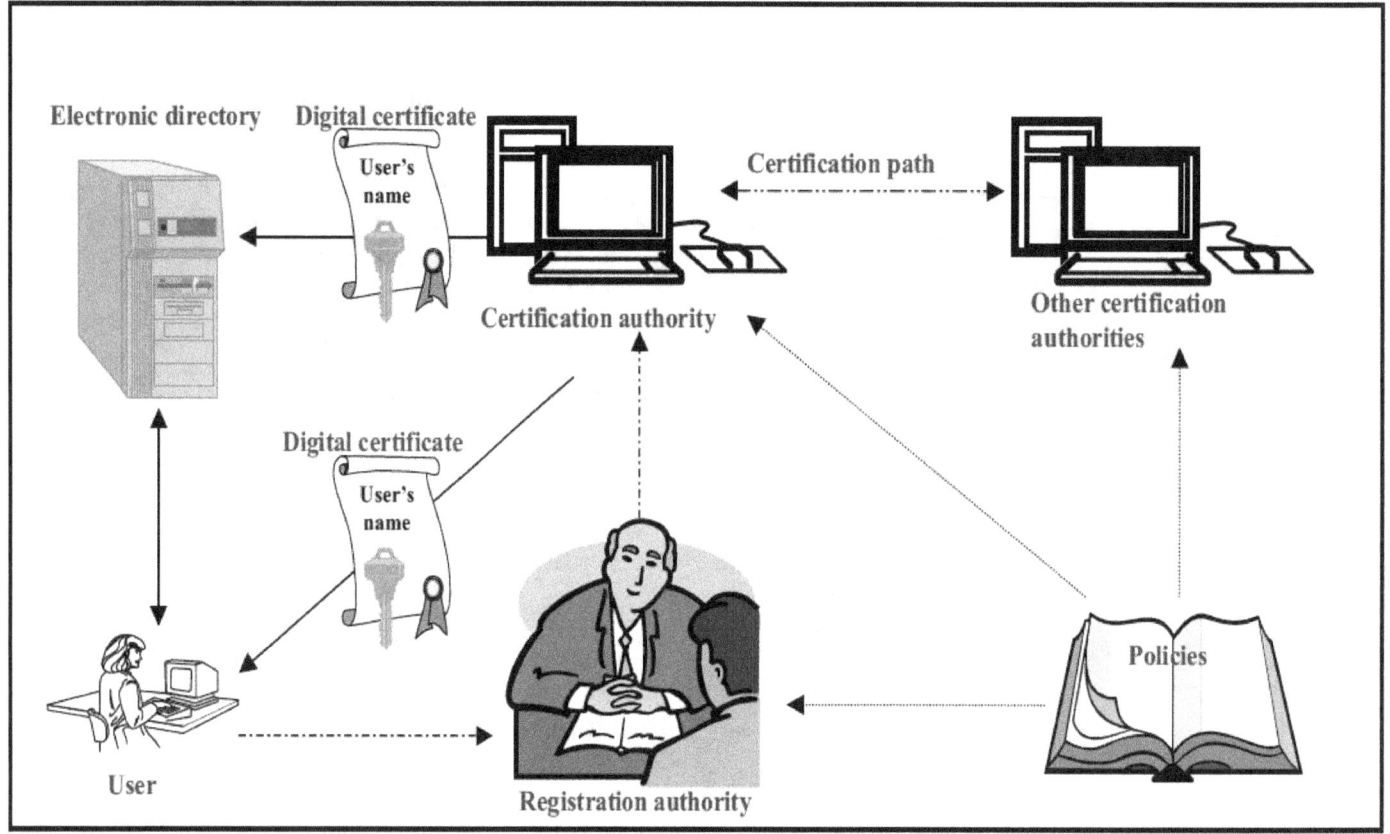

Certificates and Certification Authorities Are the Technical Mechanisms for Conveying Trust in a PKI

A digital certificate is an electronic credential that guarantees the association between a public key and a specific entity.[15] It is created by placing the entity's name, the entity's public key, and certain other identifying information in a small electronic document that is stored in a directory or other database. Directories may be publicly available repositories kept on servers that act like telephone books for users to look up others' public keys. The digital certificate itself is created by a trusted

---

[15]Certificates can be issued to computer equipment and processes as well as to individuals. For example, companies that do a lot of business over the Internet obtain digital certificates for their computer servers. These certificates are used to authenticate the servers to potential customers, who can then rely on the servers to support the secure exchange of encrypted information, such as passwords and credit card numbers.

third party called a certification authority, which digitally signs the certificate, thus providing assurance that the public key contained in the certificate does indeed belong to the individual named in the certificate.

A certification authority is responsible for managing digital certificates. The purpose of the certification authority is to oversee the generation, distribution, renewal, revocation, and suspension of digital certificates. The certification authority may set restrictions on a certificate, such as the starting date for which the certificate is valid as well as its expiration date. It is at times necessary to revoke digital certificates before their established expiration dates, for example when the certificate-holder leaves the issuing organization or when the private key is compromised. Therefore, the certification authority is also responsible for providing certificate status information and may publish a certificate revocation list in a directory or maintain an on-line status-checking mechanism. The PKI software in the user's computer can verify that the certificate is valid by first verifying that the certificate has not expired and then by assuring that it has not been revoked or suspended.

Before the certification authority can issue a certificate to a user, it must verify the user's identity in accordance with the organization's preset policies. In some cases, the certification authority is set up to perform the identification and authentication of users by itself, but often this function is delegated to separate entities called registration authorities. A user's identity is verified through one of two means, based on the level of security that is deemed necessary by the organization. In the first method, the user would need to appear in person at the registration authority and present identity documents such as a birth certificate or passport. A second, less secure method, involves the confirmation of a shared secret through an on-line application. For example, the user could verify his identity by confirming something that the agency already knows about him but which is not common knowledge, such as tax return information. After verifying the user's identity, the registration authority creates a unique user name. This unique name, which may include the user's given name, ensures that people who rely on the certificate can distinguish between several individuals with similar given names, much like an e-mail address. The certification authority then creates the certificate that irrevocably links that unique name to the user's public key.

Registration authorities focus on identifying and authenticating users; they do not sign or issue digital certificates. However, the registration authority is required to comply with preset standards for verifying a person's identity.

Because registration of large numbers of people in person can be expensive, in some situations an organization may determine that a less expensive registration process is adequate, even though the result would be a somewhat lower assurance of correct authentication. Regardless, a critical link in any PKI is the binding process used to associate the user with his or her public key.

PKIs implemented by separate organizations, such as individual federal agencies, can be combined to create a larger interconnected system, such as a governmentwide, national, or international PKI. To do this, entities within each component system need a way to reliably establish an electronic path to the certification authorities that generate digital certificates for users within the other component systems. There are three major approaches, or certification path models, for doing this. First, the *trust list method* relies on all components accepting a specific list of trusted certification authorities. This approach is used by Web browsers. Second is the *hierarchical model*, in which a single "root" certification authority issues certificates to subordinate certification authorities located in each component system. Third is a *mesh architecture*, in which nonhierarchical links are established among certification authorities in separate components that are not subordinated to each other. For a complete discussion of these three different certification path models, see appendix II.

Implementation Policies Establish Trust Levels for PKIs

Organizations may choose varying levels of trust for different kinds of transactions or other electronic functions. As noted, one organization may require users to register for their digital certificates by visiting the registration authority in person, while another may allow users to register by providing identifying information on-line. One organization may require that users protect their digital certificates with a more secure hardware device, such as smart cards, while another may be satisfied with a less secure software storage device. One organization may require that the digital certificate itself contain certain information that limits the size and scope of the electronic transaction, while another may not put any limits on the use of the certificate. Each agency will have to develop its own implementation policies to meet the requirements of its particular business model for electronic transactions using PKI, and set forth in its implementation policies what types of certificates it will issue or accept. Two documents, called the certificate policy and the certification practices statement, are usually employed to provide these policies.

The certificate policy is a set of rules governing the intended use of certificates and the level of trust that a particular PKI will support. It contains items such as the obligations of the certification authority, its liabilities and warranties, confidentiality policy, identification and authentication requirements, and details of what information will be contained in the certificates. The certificate policy provides the criteria that can be used by others to determine whether to trust certificates issued by the certification authority and is also the basis for accreditation of the certification authority.

The second document, called a certification practices statement, contains a more detailed description of the mechanics followed by a certification authority in issuing and otherwise managing certificates. It outlines the procedures used to implement the policies with regard to certificate issuance, user identification and registration, certificate lifetimes and revocation, and publishing practices for certificates and certificate revocation lists. It also states the operational practices followed by the certification authority to ensure security. The certification practices statement is used to outline operational procedures for the certification authority's personnel and also provides additional information to the relying party.

Objectives, Scope, and Methodology

Our objectives were to assess (1) the progress of the federal government in planning and coordinating federal PKI initiatives and (2) the remaining challenges to be overcome before PKI can be put into widespread use.

As background, we reviewed laws affecting federal PKI, such as the Government Paperwork Elimination Act (Public Law 105-277, October 21, 1998) and the Electronic Signatures in Global and National Commerce Act (Public Law 106-229, June 30, 2000). We also reviewed related policy and guidance, including *OMB Procedures and Guidance on Implementing the Government Paperwork Elimination Act* (OMB Memorandum M-00-10, April 25, 2000); *Federal Agency Use of Public Key Technology for Digital Signatures and Authentication* (NIST Special Publication 800-25, September 2000); *Guideline for Implementing Cryptography in the Federal Government* (NIST Special Publication 800-21, November 1999); and *Legal Considerations in Designing and Implementing Electronic Processes: A Guide for Federal Agencies* (Department of Justice, November 2000).

To evaluate what progress has been achieved on a governmentwide basis in planning and coordinating federal PKI initiatives, we reviewed documentation and held discussions with representatives of the FPKISC of the CIO Council. The FPKISC is responsible for assisting agencies in their selection and use of PKI, including supporting interagency interoperability through the FBCA, which the FPKISC has sponsored. We reviewed FPKISC documentation regarding agencies' independent PKI projects and discussed them with FPKISC representatives. We also reviewed documentation and held discussions with GSA officials who are implementing the ACES program.

Discussions with, and documents from, the FPKISC and GSA also formed the basis for how we assessed what challenges remain to be overcome in implementing PKI throughout the government. To achieve this objective we also interviewed personnel at DOD, which is implementing various PKI projects, and reviewed major pieces of its PKI documentation. In addition, we reviewed documentation on PKI prepared by technical experts, including the FPKISC Technical Working Group that is chaired by the NIST, and other organizations such as the Internet Engineering Task Force, the Giga Information Group, and the Open Group.

We performed our audit work from April 2000 through November 2000, in accordance with generally accepted government auditing standards. We requested and received comments on a draft of this report from OMB, GSA, DOD, the Chairman of the FPKISC, and Treasury. Letters from GSA and Treasury are reprinted in appendixes III and IV. Specific issues raised by reviewing agencies, along with our responses, are discussed in chapter 3.

Chapter 2

The Federal Government Has Made Progress in Planning and Coordinating PKI Initiatives

To further the development and deployment of secure electronic government, a number of public key technology initiatives have been started governmentwide as well as at individual agencies. The Federal Public Key Infrastructure Steering Committee (FPKISC) has been working to broaden awareness of the benefits of PKI technology and to promote coordination of PKI activities throughout the federal government. Most notably, the committee has developed a mechanism, the Federal Bridge Certification Authority (FBCA), to connect disparate agency PKI applications into a broader network. A prototype bridge authority has been constructed, with some of its functions already successfully tested. The Federal PKI Policy Authority will oversee and coordinate agency involvement with the bridge authority. A production version of the FBCA is under construction and is expected to be available for operation in the second quarter of fiscal year 2001.

In addition, the GSA's Access Certificates for Electronic Services (ACES) program is available to help agencies with some elements of an "off the shelf" PKI, to promote wider adoption of the technology. SSA and the Federal Emergency Management Administration, among others, are planning to make use of ACES to build PKI technology into some of their applications. Several other agencies—including DOD, DOE, FDIC, NASA, and the U.S. Patent and Trademark Office—have already implemented or are in the process of implementing PKI projects independently of ACES.

Federal PKI Steering Committee Was Established to Oversee Governmentwide PKI Efforts

The FPKISC was established in 1996 to centralize coordination and oversight of federal PKI activities. The committee is overseen by the CIO Council,[1] which is the principal interagency forum for improving practices in the design, modernization, use, sharing, and performance of federal government agency information resources. The CIO Council's mission is to promote change through consensus building and recommendations; it does not control agency decision-making processes or funding. Similarly, the FPKISC does not have the authority to compel agencies to adopt a particular PKI strategy but instead works to gain broad consensus on

---

[1]Originally the FPKISC was under the Government Information Technology Services (GITS) Board, which was established and co-chaired by OMB and the National Partnership for Reinventing Government. Because of the need to consolidate information technology improvement initiatives, the GITS Board, in February 2000, proposed to the CIO Council that its initiatives be incorporated into the council's activities, which the council endorsed. As a result, the board was dissolved in April 2000 and its initiatives, including those of the FPKISC, were folded into the federal CIO Council.

issues regarding the potential development of a federal PKI. As of December 2000, FPKISC membership consisted of 113 individuals from 27 agencies, two states, two government-chartered corporations, and one university.

The FPKISC's stated goal is to promote interoperable PKI solutions within the federal government, the development of common guidance, and the sharing of information so that agencies considering or deploying PKI solutions can benefit from those that have already done so. An example of the FPKISC's efforts to develop common guidance is the committee's recent assistance to OMB in drafting guidelines for implementing the Government Paperwork Elimination Act. Most of the committee's work is carried out by three working groups devoted to legal and policy issues, business issues, and technical issues, respectively. Through monthly meetings of the steering committee and its working groups, the FPKISC provides a forum through which agency representatives can learn about what other agencies are doing, share experiences, and ask for assistance.

Administration of the FPKISC's activities has been overseen by a chair and four staff members—two detailees from the National Security Agency, one detailee from SSA, and one contract employee. The salaries of the chair and the contract employee are paid from funds set aside for the Key Recovery Demonstration Project, which was provided by the National Security Agency and other agencies, and is administered through the Department of the Treasury. For fiscal year 2001, staffing of the FPKISC has declined to one chair and two staff members—one agency detailee and one contract employee. FPKISC officials, acting through the CIO Council, have requested about $500,000 for fiscal year 2001. However, if the number of agencies or other parties applying for participation with the FBCA increases, the need for resources to review those applications may also grow, as will the need for resources to perform additional administrative functions, such as notifications and postings.

The FPKISC Has Taken Steps to Link Individual Agency PKIs Into a Federal PKI

The FPKISC has worked to develop a mechanism to link individual agency PKIs into a single federal structure. Originally the FPKISC advocated a hierarchical certification path model with a single root federal certification authority that would issue certificates to all federal agencies, which would in turn issue certificates to their subordinate offices and divisions and, finally, to their employees, trading partners, and members of the public.

This is the approach currently being implemented by the Government of Canada.[2] However, a number of PKI initiatives had already begun in various agencies of the government, and the FPKISC did not have the authority to direct a governmentwide, top-down approach for PKI. In the committee's view, too many agencies had independently begun to test their own individual PKI applications, and too many vendors had introduced disparate products and services to the marketplace. As a result, the committee began working on a looser structure that would attempt to meld disparate individual agency PKI projects, supported by a variety of commercial vendors, into a broad, interoperable network.

The keystone of the FPKISC's approach is the FBCA, shown in figure 7. With the creation of the FBCA, the federal government has taken an important first step in the development of a federal PKI. The FBCA is designed to facilitate certificate validation and cross-certification among both federal and nonfederal certification authorities, including state and local government agencies and the private sector.

---

[2]For additional information, see Government of Canada, Communications Security Establishment, *Government of Canada Public Key Infrastructure White Paper,* February 1998.

Figure 7: FBCA Certification Path Model

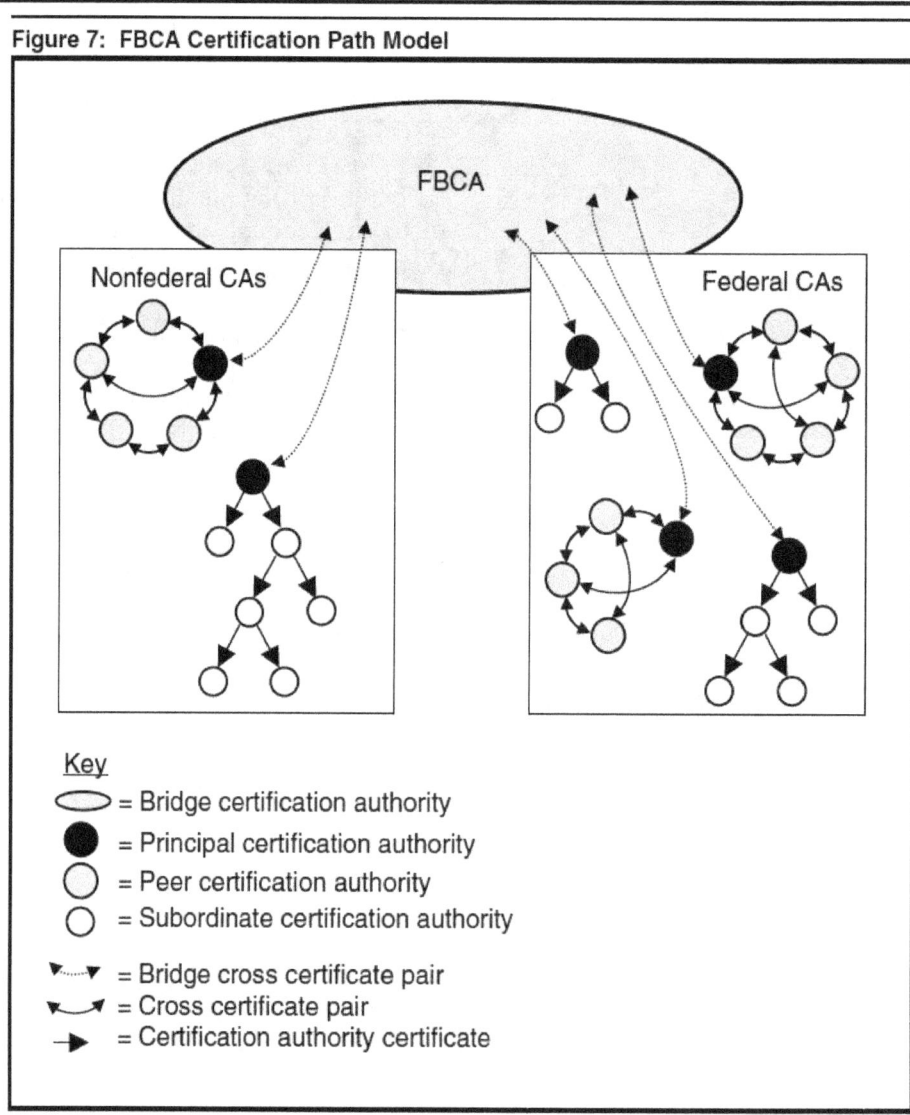

Source: Federal Public Key Infrastructure Steering Committee.

A prototype FBCA was tested in April 2000 at the annual conference of the Electronic Messaging Association. The prototype demonstrated digital signature certificate interoperability on several levels—between five different certification authority products, five different directories, and two different e-mail applications. (See figure 8.) The organizations that participated were the National Institute of Standards and Technology, NASA, the National Security Agency, the Georgia Tech Research Institute (GTRI), and the Government of Canada. According to the chairman of the

FPKISC, the demonstration successfully validated signature certifications through complex chains of certification authorities, including some that were up to seven certification authorities in length.

Figure 8: FBCA Demonstration Certification Path

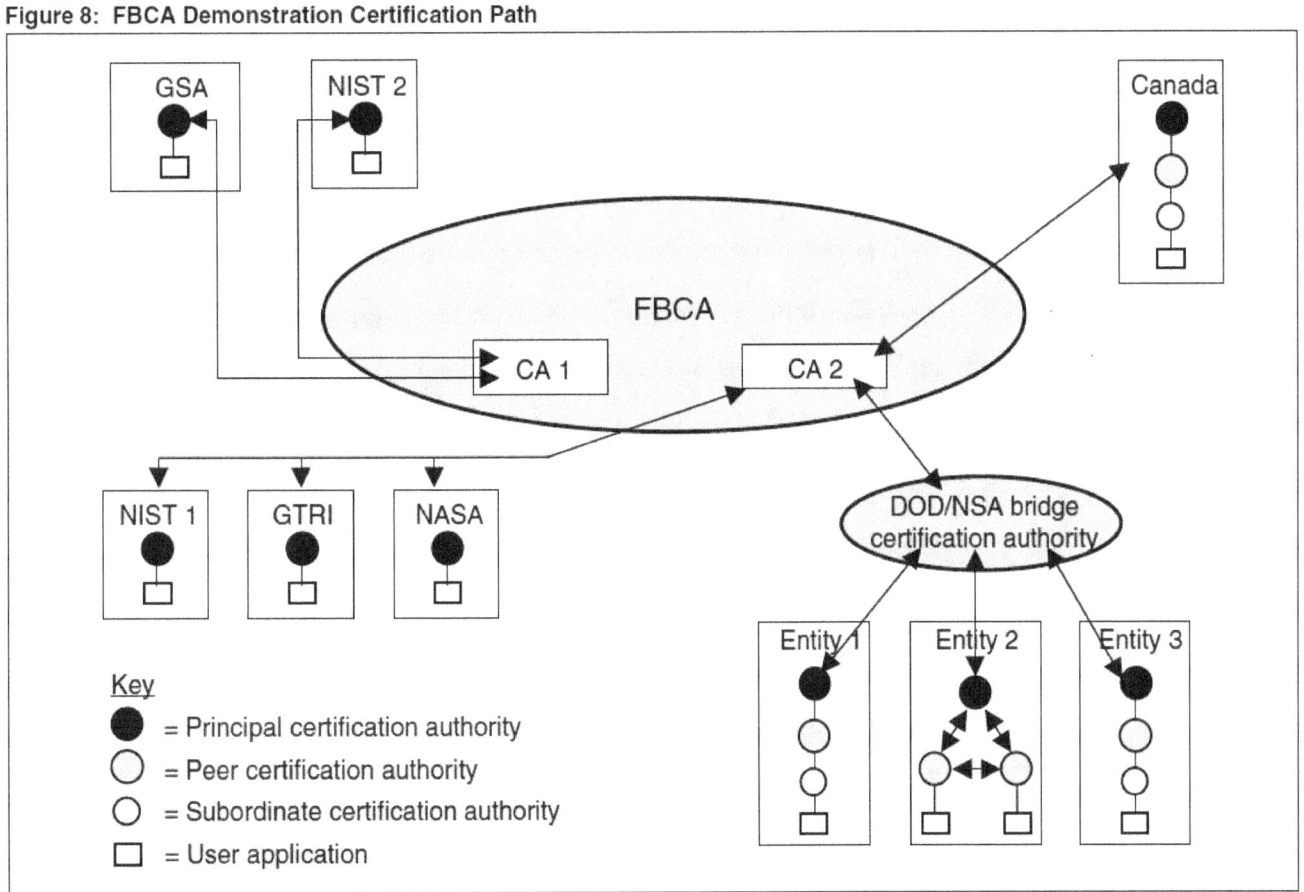

Source: Federal Public Key Infrastructure Steering Committee.

A primary function of the FBCA will be to attempt to reconcile the varying trust levels that agencies will inevitably establish for their different PKIs. An agency that has developed a PKI to help protect a very sensitive function will not want to connect to the federal PKI unless it can be assured that any external certificates it accepts also meet the same strict assurance requirements that it has established internally. Otherwise, the security of its system could be compromised simply because another interconnected agency has not maintained adequate internal security policies and procedures. However, not all agencies will likely require the same trust levels for all their applications. Agencies who have less stringent security needs may set lower trust levels for their PKIs because it will likely be less expensive for them to do so. For this reason, varying trust levels among agencies is probably unavoidable, and procedures are required to ensure that each component PKI accepts only the proper kind of certificates.

The FBCA is taking steps to address this and other issues that arise when attempting to interconnect disparate agency PKIs. When processing certificates, the FBCA will provide information on each certificate's trust level, as well as verifying its source and status, so that the receiving agency's PKI can determine whether the certificate meets its requirements. To perform this function, a set of standard trust levels has been set for the FBCA, and a Federal PKI Policy Authority has been established to correlate each participating agency PKI's trust level with one of the FBCA's standard levels. For each of its standard trust levels, the policy authority will establish guidelines for operating certification authorities and procedures for monitoring compliance with those guidelines, such as annual compliance audits, to ensure that the certification authorities continue to maintain the advertised trust levels. Agencies will also be required to meet additional interoperability requirements, such as compliance with the federal certificate profile, which specifies how digital certificates should be constructed.

GSA's ACES Program Is Designed to Foster PKI Use by Agencies

GSA has also worked to promote federal agency adoption of PKI technology. Its Office of Information Security built the prototype FBCA and is expected to build and manage the operational version. Additionally, since 1996, GSA's Federal Technology Service has sponsored a separate program designed to develop and provide some of the elements of an "off the shelf" PKI to individual agencies to promote wider adoption of the technology. As stated, the ACES project is focused on government transactions made directly with the general public.

The intent of ACES is to provide public key certificates to individual citizens to use when accessing and submitting information electronically with the government. GSA expects that ACES will provide an expandable foundation that will be collectively used by federal agencies, thus stimulating the widespread use of a uniform PKI, promoting interoperability among agency PKI implementations, and achieving cost savings throughout the government.

As of October 1999, GSA made awards to three prime contractors to provide a range of services to any agency wishing to implement PKI technology. At the most basic level, the contractors can provide digital signature certificates to agencies without their having to develop their own PKIs. For each certificate, agencies will be charged an issuance fee—which varies depending on which ACES contractor is issuing the certificate and that currently could be as high as $18.00—and a transaction fee ranging from 40¢ to $1.20 each time the certificate is used. Agencies will have to determine which applications are best suited to use ACES certificates. For example, GSA officials have stated that it would probably not be cost-effective to use ACES for less sensitive, high-volume applications, such as electronic mail. In order to jump-start the use of ACES certificates by agencies of the federal government, in May 2000 GSA announced that 500,000 ACES certificates would be distributed to agencies free of the normal issuance costs. More advanced PKI services are also available through the ACES contractors, including the creation of an agency-specific, customized PKI; consulting services for developing certificate policies and certification practices statements; development of ACES-enabled applications and encryption services; and smart-card technology.

Although the goal of ACES is to motivate and facilitate agencies to use PKI technology to provide electronic services to the public and business, few agencies have been willing to be in the forefront of introducing electronic service delivery. As of November 2000, only seven task orders had been issued for ACES services, and only two agencies had taken advantage of GSA's offer of free certificates. It remains to be seen to what extent agencies are motivated to use ACES to advance their PKI applications for two reasons. First, ACES allows users to apply on-line for their digital certificates, rather than apply in person. Agencies that are considering using ACES for sensitive applications may determine that on-line identity binding is not secure enough for their purposes. For example, according to a DOD official, the certificates issued under the ACES contract do not meet DOD's requirements for face-to-face registration. Second, it is unclear whether agencies will be willing to support the fee-for-certificate-use cost model that is projected to be a major source of revenue for ACES contractors.

Independent PKI Projects Are Under Way at Other Agencies

PKI projects are currently being funded independently at a number of federal agencies, including DOD, DOE, FDIC, NASA, and the U.S. Patent and Trademark Office. PKIs are being used for a variety of applications, especially those involving personnel matters, contracts, and financial transfers. These include pilot projects as well as operational applications. Generally speaking, federal agency efforts to date have focused on using PKI technology for transactions (1) within individual agencies, (2) between two or more different agencies, and (3) between agencies and their commercial trading partners.

Two major PKI applications being developed at DOD are the Defense Message System (DMS) and the Defense Travel System (DTS). DMS is an organizational and individual messaging service accessible from personal computers at DOD locations around the world, including those of tactically deployed personnel and other U.S. government users, with interfaces to Allied users and DOD contractors. DMS will replace DOD's aging automatic digital network system, which required special, separate terminals to send and receive messages. As of November 2000, almost all of the unclassified and secret sites that had been scheduled to implement DMS had been commissioned for operations.

The second effort, DTS, is a new, paperless travel system that allows the traveler to coordinate and arrange temporary duty business travel more quickly and easily than the existing system. Travelers will no longer have to go to separate offices to get travel orders, travel advances, transportation, lodging, and rental car arrangements. Under DTS, all of these transactions can be made securely from a desktop or laptop computer. Once the completed travel voucher is digitally signed by the traveler and approved by the authorizing officer, the system will issue payments to the traveler and the government credit card company. A limited operational test of DTS began in October 2000, and the data from that test are currently being analyzed. While the primary driver for DOD's development of PKI has been to improve security of transactions rather than promote electronic government, these projects are also intended to result in major business improvements for DOD.

According to the FPKISC, DOE has several ongoing applications that employ PKI. Five certification authorities have cross-certified among themselves at DOE national laboratories and field activities, with over 2,000 certificates issued to DOE federal and contractor employees in support of secure and authenticated e-mail, file management, data transfers, and personnel management functions. An additional 500 certificates were expected to be issued in fiscal year 2000. Additionally, DOE is performing a pilot project in support of travel requests and travel claims processing. The department is in the process of designing a headquarters PKI, with the goal of interoperating with the existing laboratory and field activity PKIs.

FDIC implemented two separate PKIs, one a low-assurance PKI and the second a medium-assurance PKI. The low-assurance PKI is used for SSL Web-based applications on its extranet with member institutions and external parties, such as state and federal regulatory agencies. The medium-assurance PKI is used by FDIC employees and some contractors for digitally signing and encrypting electronic travel vouchers to facilitate processing.

NASA is currently working on an agencywide PKI for a variety of applications that support the agency's mission. Planned uses of PKI include encrypting and digitally signing e-mail, encrypting files on desktops, and securing Web transactions. NASA is considering numerous other uses for PKI, including financial management, electronic grants, electronic forms, firewalls, and virtual private networks. The NASA PKI will have to support diverse headquarters and center environments, consisting of networked Intel-compatible, Apple, and Unix workstations, as well as some stand-alone workstations in laboratories or special operational environments.

The U.S. Patent and Trademark Office of the Department of Commerce has two applications in use that take advantage of PKI technology. The Patent Application Information Retrieval System, which is currently operational, permits authenticated access to the status of patent application information using a digital signature. In June 2000, there were 40,872 reported secure queries to the system. And in October 2000, an Electronic Patent Application Filing System went operational to provide inventors with the capability to file an application for a new invention with the U.S. Patent and Trademark Office, in which PKI technology was used to guarantee the security of electronic applications. To date, over $4 million has been spent on these PKI programs. This represents a considerable investment, but the Patent Office believes that it will translate into substantial savings and improved service delivery.

Chapter 3

Full PKI Implementation Faces Many Formidable Challenges

While progress in spreading PKI technology throughout the government is ongoing, the fact remains that designing and building full-featured PKI implementations remains a difficult challenge. While user application software with some public key features, such as the secure sockets layer (SSL) protocol, is now in widespread use, full-featured PKI implementations are not yet commonplace in either the government or the private sector. A number of substantial issues must be addressed before the technology can be widely and effectively deployed.

- Current PKI products and implementations suffer from significant interoperability problems, which make it difficult for agency officials to make decisions about how to develop a PKI.
- Because full-featured PKIs are rare, and those that exist are in the early stages of implementation and use, questions remain about how well this technology will truly scale and interoperate as its use grows.
- Adoption of the technology may be impeded by the high costs that, to date, have been associated with building a PKI and enabling software applications to use it.
- An effective PKI—at any level within the government—will require a well-defined set of policies for ensuring that stipulated levels of trust are maintained on an ongoing basis. Establishing those policies will require resolution of a range of historically sensitive issues and thus may be difficult.
- Finally, as with any security technology, the success of a PKI will depend on how well people interact with the system and how well it is implemented. Thus, federal agencies, which do not have a strong track record[1] in managing information security, will be faced with the challenge of training and involving systems administrators as well as users in the adoption of a technology that many find complex and difficult to understand.

To date, federal agencies have not been directed by any governmentwide standards for developing and managing PKIs. The uncertainties and risks the government faces could be mitigated by establishing and enforcing an overall management framework for implementing PKI within the federal government. Such a framework would define roles and responsibilities for the development and management of the federal PKI, identify required

---

[1]*Information Security: Serious and Widespread Weaknesses Persist at Federal Agencies* (GAO/AIMD-00-295, September 6, 2000) and *Federal Information Security: Actions Needed to Address Widespread Weaknesses* (GAO/T/AIMD-00-135, March 29, 2000).

resources, and set policies to provide a consistent direction to individual agencies. The framework could also include a governmentwide PKI architecture, which would provide a technical structure for implementing PKIs, thus reducing the risk of agencies building systems that are noninteroperable and unnecessarily costly to maintain.

Interoperability Problems Make Broad Deployment Decisions Difficult

Although vendors have generally designed and developed PKI products based on existing standards, those standards are not always clear and fully defined, leaving vendors to devise their own interpretations of the requirements and in most cases develop their own proprietary approaches to nonstandardized functions. The lack of interoperability among PKI products leaves federal planners with several problems.

- *Choosing among multiple noninteroperable products means taking the risk of adopting an approach that does not fully conform to standards and may soon need to be replaced.* Although standards bodies, such as the Internet Engineering Task Force (IETF) and others, have developed and published a wide spectrum of public key technology standards to support various aspects of PKI implementation, these standards are not always complete enough to ensure interoperability. Thus, in some cases, commercial vendors claim they have developed PKI products based on published standards, yet their products still cannot work with those of other companies. Although a standard should provide a common specification of syntax and semantics for implementing a particular function, the description might not be precise enough. Some semantics may be missing or incompletely defined, or aspects of the standard may be misinterpreted or implemented improperly, which can lead to noninteroperable systems.

  A prime example is the X.509 version 3 standard for digital certificates. The standard defines various aspects of how certificates are to be constructed and managed, including what data fields are to be required and what information will be in them. The standard also includes some optional data fields that can be used for other attributes not defined in the standard. Because the predefined data fields do not cover all the attributes that some PKI implementers need, the optional fields have been used for this additional information. A consistent approach for using the optional fields in the X.509 standard can significantly improve certificate interoperability. An application can accept certificates from multiple certification authorities only if the certificates conform to a consistent certificate profile for their optional fields. However, if the optional fields are used in different ways by different PKI implementations, the certificates they produce cannot be interchanged without risk of improperly processing the added information.

The National Institute of Standards and Technology (NIST) has developed a federal certificate profile that agencies wishing to interoperate with the FBCA can use in developing their PKI implementations. The federal certificate profile defines which extensions may be used, the interpretations for those extensions, and how data are populated in those fields. It does not preclude the use of additional extensions, but it does define a consistent way of using and interpreting several extensions considered essential to interoperability with the FBCA. However, agencies are not required to conform with the federal certificate profile if they do not plan to participate in the FBCA.

- *The FBCA, which may help link some disparate agency PKIs developed from noninteroperable products, is not yet operational.* The FBCA is designed to allow valid certificates generated in one agency's PKI to be accepted by another agency's PKI, assuming that both agencies have agreed in advance to have their PKIs bridged by the FBCA. The FBCA's solution avoids the problem of interoperability among incompatible PKI products by essentially translating the information in agency-specific digital certificates into common terms that can be understood by the other participating agency PKIs—a process known as certificate policy mapping. However, the production version of the FBCA is not yet operational, and current PKI products do not support direct interaction between agencies' PKIs. Furthermore, the certificate policy mapping function is not yet in operation and will not be truly tested until multiple agencies field PKIs and attempt to have them interoperate through the FBCA. As a result, the success of the FBCA in overcoming interoperability problems and stimulating broad adoption of PKI technology in the federal government is not yet assured.

- *Directory interoperability, which is critical to the sharing of certificate information within a PKI or network of PKIs, is difficult to engineer.* On-line directories serve the workhorse function of communicating with users on a continuing basis to identify public keys and confirm their validity. However, in many cases, directories do not work with each other because directory products are implemented and configured differently. For example, they may not use the same scheme to keep track of the names of files and other electronic entities. If software on one user's computer cannot find the information it needs in another agency's directory (because the information may be organized differently in that directory or because the directory was implemented based on a different protocol), then secure transactions cannot take place between the user and that other agency.

Within the federal government, the de facto federal PKI distributed directory system will consist of an FBCA directory and a number of disparate PKI domain directories. As a result of directory interoperability difficulties identified during the prototype FBCA demonstration held in April 2000, an ad hoc federal PKI Directory Working Group was formed in June 2000 under the FPKISC to develop a directory profile that outlines the requirements for agencies to interoperate with the FBCA and its directory. To date, the working group developed a draft directory profile, and ongoing meetings are scheduled for further discussion.

- *The lack of widely accepted standard application programming interfaces (API) forces PKI application developers to rely on vendor-specific tool kits or government-issued software modules, which are also likely to limit the interoperability of the resulting applications.* Even when the PKI-specific components of a system have been made to successfully interoperate with other systems, the task still remains to communicate the information processed by the PKI with the user applications that rely on it. Currently, vendors provide product-specific tool kits,[2] which are used to modify user software applications so that they will interact correctly with a specific PKI implementation. Although several API standards have been developed, none of them is widely accepted, and vendor tool kits are not based on them. Thus, a tool kit from one vendor will enable an application to work only with a PKI implemented using that particular vendor's products. Agencies cannot replace one vendor's PKI product with a product from a different vendor and expect the application to continue to work.

Using a standard API to adapt applications to use PKIs could eliminate the need for vendor tool kits and reduce development costs and implementation time frames. This approach has already worked in specific cases at the agency level. For example, the Army Corps of Engineers developed and deployed an electronic signature system

---

[2]A vendor-provided tool kit is used to develop applications that require encryption, decryption, digital signature, and other cryptographic operations. The tool kit is usually based on proprietary interfaces that only work with one vendor's solution.

using high-level APIs. The Department of State was able to adopt this same system for an application it was developing, saving an estimated $750,000 and accelerating the project's implementation by about 30 months.[3]

The cumulative effect of these interoperability problems is to make it difficult for agency officials to make decisions about how to develop a PKI using currently available commercial products and for application vendors to tailor their products to use PKI technology. Agencies run the risk of developing a system that does not work with existing applications or other PKI systems and that may require extensive and costly modifications to meet agency objectives. It is very likely that some noninteroperable PKI products currently in use will quickly become obsolete and need to be replaced. In addition, without an established set of high-level APIs that vendors could build into their applications, the availability of applications that are PKI-compliant is limited because it may not be cost-effective to build an interface for the various PKI products that are available.

Most PKIs Have Been Limited to Pilot Projects or Specific Applications

Agencies of the federal government have only limited experience with PKI, and much of it is based on pilot projects or relatively small-scale applications. Because of this limited practical experience, it is not known how well PKI technology can be scaled to the level of hundreds of thousands or even millions of users, as will be encountered in a fully operational, interconnected PKI serving the entire federal government. The mechanisms needed to support a large-scale implementation of PKI may not work well in an environment supporting operations of the entire federal government, its trading partners, and the public.

Most PKI projects at individual agencies have been limited to relatively small pilot projects or specific applications. For example, the Patent Office's Electronic Patent Application Filing System is targeted to a relatively small population of patent attorneys. As of August 11, 2000, the system had been deployed to 14 law firms, one independent inventor, and one corporation. It had issued 1,032 certificates. Another example is the National Institutes of Health, which developed a PKI for secure electronic mail. At the time of our review, about 500 certificates had been issued for the National Institutes of Health PKI, with plans to expand to about 15,000

---

[3]*Electronic Signature: Sanction of the Department of State's System* (GAO/AIMD-00-227R, July 10, 2000).

certificates by the middle of 2001. DOD implemented a medium-assurance PKI in July 2000 and is planning to issue certificates on common access cards to all DOD personnel by October 2002, perhaps ultimately affecting as much as half the federal work force.

Efforts to develop a governmentwide PKI are also still in the very early phases, and concrete results have yet to emerge. To handle the large and diverse population of federal employees, business partners, and public citizens that will be encompassed by a federal PKI, a network of trusted registration authorities will be needed to verify the identities of all users in a rigorous and consistent way. In addition, another vast network of interoperable on-line directories will need to be in place so that every user's identity can be looked up and his or her digital certificate verified before any transaction takes place. Software applications will potentially have to consult a number of disparate directories to work out a trust path that can be used to validate an incoming user's digital certificate. Significant problems with verification failures or unacceptably slow response times are quite possible until further operational experience is gained.

The prototype FBCA has only been demonstrated in a laboratory environment, as opposed to full-scale testing or operational use, and it experienced very slow response times when first demonstrated in April 2000. While the FBCA is necessary in facilitating cross-certification of disparate agency PKIs, it needs to overcome a number of issues and therefore is still an immature solution. For example, because agency PKIs are not required to conform to a standard and are also likely to constantly change, a continual effort will be needed to map changing agency policies to the FBCA's predefined trust levels. This policy mapping activity, as well as certification path creation for encryption certificates, was not demonstrated at the April 2000 test. A DOD bridge certification authority technology demonstration, featuring certificate policy mapping and other capabilities, is currently planned for February 2001. Upon completing the demonstration, the functions will be used to support the production FBCA implementation.

Similarly, ACES, GSA's project to help jump start agency adoption of PKI for public service delivery, was only beginning operational use in the fall of 2000. At the time of our review, only a handful of agencies were participating in the ACES program, and these projects were still in the early phases of implementation.

Developing and Maintaining a PKI Can Be Expensive

A significant cost is involved in developing, fielding, and maintaining a production PKI. Systems must be set up to positively identify internal and external users, issue them digital certificates, and manage the exchange and verification of certificates. In addition, existing software applications, electronic directories, and other legacy systems must be modified so they can interact with the PKI. Furthermore, outside vendors that conduct electronic business with an agency will likely incur costs and disruption to make their own systems compatible. As a result, the total cost associated with building a PKI and enabling applications to use it can be significant.

Agencies that are developing their own enterprisewide PKIs need to consider the cost associated with enabling their applications to use a PKI as well as the cost of developing the PKI itself. A PKI by itself offers no value until it is paired with applications designed to make use of its security services. For example, an e-mail application must be PKI-enabled to encrypt/decrypt and digitally sign messages as well as to retrieve and validate certificates from distributed directories in order to achieve authentication, confidentiality, integrity, and nonrepudiation. DOD, for instance, has identified a need for $170 million to initially modify some applications to work with its PKI. This is in addition to the approximately $700 million from fiscal year 2000 through fiscal year 2005 that the department has requested solely for PKI development. To date, DOD has identified about 600 applications—of which only a limited number will be modified with this funding—throughout the military services as candidates for PKI, out of approximately 9,000 to 10,000 systems that were considered. If DOD decides to PKI-enable more systems, a significant additional cost will be incurred.

Another issue that agencies have to address is the cost to outside contractors of interacting with an agency's PKI in order to conduct electronic business. Vendors may incur significant costs in obtaining digital certificates to conduct business with the federal government. Although this is not a direct cost to the agencies, the financial impact to the vendors may have an indirect impact on the cost of agency programs. And the financial impact is compounded if vendors must modify their systems to deal effectively with multiple agencies that may have implemented multiple incompatible PKIs. DOD has established external certification authorities, which are authorized to sell digital certificates that work with the DOD PKI. Non-DOD organizations that wish to do business with DOD need to buy certificates from one of these authorities. The cost per certificate is about $200, and only a few contractors have purchased certificates from the external certification authorities. DOD is aware of this issue and hopes to reduce the cost per certificate in order to encourage participation from non-DOD organizations in its electronic business activities.

Policy Issues Can Be Difficult to Resolve

As discussed, implementing a PKI involves more than just installing and configuring the system's technical components. It is equally necessary to establish the assurance objectives to be achieved by the PKI and policies and procedures to support those objectives. The process of establishing a complete set of policies to support a PKI can involve addressing a number of difficult issues, including the following.

- *Privacy.* The public has shown that while it is increasingly willing to use the Internet to transact business, it is concerned about controlling when, how, and to what extent personal information is collected and used.[4] If the federal PKI is not properly implemented and managed, the technologies that have been developed to manage massive volumes of personal information could also be abused. It is no longer technically difficult for the government to establish databases that collect extensive personal information about large numbers of individual citizens. There is a growing sense that too much data have been computerized while few safeguards have been established. In many transactions, it is important that the least amount of information be required and provided so as to preserve privacy. This means that when technologies such as PKI are implemented, extra care must be taken to avoid improperly gathering or using personal information.
- *Maintaining assurance (trust) levels.* Having established a certain level of trust for a PKI, an agency will have to develop implementation policies for establishing and maintaining that trust level. For example, policies are needed that focus on issues such as what assurance information will be included in digital certificates, how individual users will obtain digital certificates, and how user private keys will be protected. The higher the level of trust, the more stringent the process of user identification that will be required to create and assign digital certificates. If users are to present positive identification in person in order to get their certificates, for example, then registration authorities must be set up with trained, trusted personnel to operate them. If smart

---

[4]See *Internet Privacy: Federal Agency Use of Cookies* (GAO-01-147R, October 20, 2000) and *Internet Privacy: Agencies' Efforts to Implement OMB's Privacy Policy* (GAO/GGD-00-191, September 5, 2000).

cards are to be used to protect users' private keys, a process to distribute and manage the smart cards will be necessary. Furthermore, the agency will have to develop a policy for determining whether to interconnect with other PKIs and accept their digital certificates. Most important, once the appropriate policies and procedures have been developed and implemented, an additional process will be needed to ensure that required assurance levels do not degrade over time. For example, agencies may be required to conduct periodic audits of their PKIs to ensure that policies and procedures are being followed.

- *Encryption key recovery.* If the keying material associated with the encrypted data becomes lost or unusable for any reason, then those data will be effectively lost unless some means exists to recover the keying material. Accordingly, agencies will need to establish policies on escrowing and distributing the keying material necessary to recover such data.

- *Long-term proof of identity and authenticity.* Agencies will need to develop policies for electronically archiving digitally signed documents possibly for long periods of time. Public key certificates, even very old ones, will be maintained in association with electronic documents for the long term, and the ability to properly process the security information and maintain the level of assurance will also have to be preserved. Agencies may have to produce these business documents under subpoena, thus requiring a process for tamper-proof audit trails to show that the integrity of the data is assured. In addition to digital signature verification, agencies will also have to address other related issues, such as maintaining the validity and security of transaction time stamps and other requirements for legal proof.

Because all of these issues have significant resource and organizational implications, the process of establishing and maintaining appropriate policies and procedures will likely be very challenging for any agency attempting to develop a full-featured PKI.

Organizationwide Training Will Be Vital to Successful PKI Implementation

PKI technology is complex and difficult to grasp. As with any other technology used to provide security, the assurance provided by a PKI will be only as good as the practices and procedures of the users and administrators who maintain the system on a daily basis. For example, if administrators do not properly configure and maintain the PKI software and hardware, vulnerabilities may be exposed that an attacker could exploit. Likewise, if users do not properly safeguard their private keys, or do not know how to properly interact with the PKI functions in their application software, other vulnerabilities will be opened for potential exploitation.

A PKI that otherwise would offer a high level of security could face significant vulnerabilities if administrators do not properly configure system servers and other devices. Even a very well-designed and implemented PKI will lose its effectiveness if users do not properly safeguard their private keys or do not understand the inherent vulnerabilities associated with Web browsers, such as improperly accepting unverified certificates. As a result, each agency implementing and deploying a PKI must ensure that appropriate training and support is available for management, staff, and users throughout the life of the project. And users must be trained in how to use applications that have been modified to work with digital certificates.

According to a report published by the Giga Information Group, a contributing factor to the lack of adoption of PKI technology thus far is that early adopters of PKI have found it difficult for users to interact with PKI systems.[5] Tasks such as generating private/public key pairs, protecting private keys, and backing up and using digital certificates may be difficult for users to understand. While it is important to hide as many of the technical details of PKI functions as possible from users, it remains important that users understand what is happening when the PKI software responds unexpectedly, such as when a certificate has been rejected or is no longer valid or a digital signature does not match the original. Users will need to be trained in what actions to take in response to these events, which they may find frustrating because they will likely be prevented from carrying out their intended business. Developing and implementing an effective training program will contribute to the cost and time involved in developing a PKI.

---

[5]Giga Information Group, *Cost and Difficulties in User Understanding Are the Main Barriers to Digital Certificate Adoption*, November 29, 1999.

Current Agency Initiatives Are Not Guided by a Federal PKI Management Framework

Resolving the range of PKI implementation challenges will be no trivial task for federal agencies; no simple solutions are available. However, most of these challenges involve uncertainty about what standard management approaches and technical solutions the government is likely to adopt. Without being overly prescriptive, a well-defined management framework for the federal government's PKI efforts would provide guidance that could mitigate some of the risk that agencies face in adopting PKI technology.

To date, federal agencies have not been directed by any governmentwide standards for developing and managing PKIs. Early agency PKI pilot projects have been focused on narrow communities of interest and have not addressed larger compatibility problems. Although the FPKISC has acknowledged the "need for a thoughtful, overarching mechanism to help ensure the interoperable use of such technology" in the federal government, the committee does not provide top-down policy guidance to agencies on developing and implementing PKIs and has not developed or sponsored an official federal PKI management framework.[6] All FPKISC guidance is strictly for optional use by federal agencies. Since 1998 the committee has taken a "governance by the governed" approach, in which agencies implementing PKIs collectively determine how best to ensure efficient and seamless interoperability.

A management framework would provide complete, integrated guidance to federal agencies that could help them to lessen the risks involved in deciding to adopt PKI technology. Such a framework would also promote interoperability among agencies' PKIs and thus further development of a federal governmentwide PKI. Essential elements of a management framework that are not currently well defined are discussed below.

- *A program plan identifying roles and responsibilities at the governmentwide and agency levels—as well as general time frames and resources to develop, deploy, and maintain a federal PKI—has not been developed.* To date, agencies individually determine when and how to implement PKIs and what agency functions to include. The FPKISC, which serves as a "champion" for PKI issues and is in charge of planning and developing governmentwide PKI capabilities, has no directive authority. Although the FPKISC has collected information on and coordinated federal PKI efforts, it has not been in a position to provide

---

[6]FPKISC, *The Evolving Federal Public Key Infrastructure*, June 2000, p. 12.

focus to these efforts by establishing well-defined goals and time frames and highlighting required resources to achieve them, including resources for key supporting activities, such as training. This stands in contrast with other government initiatives, such as the High Performance Computing and Communications Initiative, first organized in fiscal year 1992, under which annual supplements to the President's Budget have been prepared that list specific performance goals, target dates, and funds to be earmarked throughout the government.

In this regard, some PKI planning has been done at the agency level. Specifically, DOD has developed a PKI roadmap and implementation plan that set goals and time frames and identified the roles and responsibilities for its PKI effort in areas such as program management, requirements identification, interoperability, systems development, procurement, operations, and oversight.[7] However, analogous documents have not yet been produced for the federal government as a whole.

- *Policy standards to minimize the development of unique PKI solutions by federal agencies have not been established.* At present, each federal agency develops its own PKI and management policies. As a result, agencies independently establish PKIs using different—or in some cases undefined—approaches in key implementation areas, such as privacy protection, trust levels, encryption key recovery, and long-term proof of identity and authenticity. Although PKI development is still at an early stage, basic management incompatibilities have already arisen. For example, DOD officials stated that the business model adopted by the ACES project, which is based on agencies paying a fee to a contractor every time a user's certificate is validated, would be extremely difficult to implement within DOD.

  A crucial problem is that the different levels of trust and associated means of confirming users' identities and issuing certificates that are being established at different agencies exacerbate interoperability problems. A federal certificate policy standard that agencies must adhere to currently does not exist. (Adherence to the federal certificate profile, developed by NIST, is only required of agencies participating in

---

[7]*Public Key Infrastructure Roadmap for the Department of Defense* (Version 3.0, October 29,1999) and *Public Key Infrastructure Implementation Plan for the Department of Defense* (Version 3.1, December 18, 2000).

the FBCA project.) As a result, agencies have no clear guidance on (1) what certificate classes (trust levels) will be supported across the government, (2) the binding requirements between users and their public keys for each class, (3) how key pairs are to be generated and managed, and (4) requirements for complying with existing standards, such as Federal Information Processing Standards Publication 140-1 for cryptographic modules. The policies issued by DOD and the Government of Canada are good examples of how a certificate policy could be constructed and could serve as a starting point for a governmentwide standard.

- *Technical standards—including a federal PKI architecture—that can guide the development and integration of agency PKIs are not complete.* As discussed, individual agency PKIs are not interoperable, and the FBCA has been established as a way to help bridge disparate PKIs. Without a well-defined federal PKI architecture, it is difficult to have a complete set of technical requirements that would help ensure governmentwide interoperability. Such an architecture would not preclude agencies from tailoring PKIs to meet their specific needs and could be designed to be flexible to accommodate future growth. Table 1 provides a summary of the advantages and disadvantages of having an architecture for systems development; these are analogous to the issues associated with building a federal PKI. The advantages of having an architecture are compelling, but developing an architecture will not be easy. If an architecture is to be effectively developed, maintained, and enforced, an effort will be required to reach broad agreement on the architecture, and in some cases the architecture may not support optimal solutions for all applications.

Table 1: The Advantages and Disadvantages of an Architecture

Advantages	Disadvantages
Facilitates a disciplined approach to software systems development.	Requires agreement among industry, government, and users on the elements of the architecture, which may be difficult and time-consuming to obtain.
Facilitates standard system design and development decisions that can result in reduced cost and increased performance.	
Reduces the risk of building and buying systems that are duplicative, incompatible, and costly to maintain.	Requires compliance with an overall architecture, but this may not necessarily provide an optimum solution for all applications.
Promotes systems interoperability, portability, and scalability.	
Provides flexibility to accommodate future growth.	
Can reduce reliance on proprietary solutions.	

According to its strategic plan for fiscal years 2001 through 2002, the federal CIO Council, which oversees the FPKISC, is aware of the need for a framework of policies and guidance for federal PKI efforts. The council's stated goals are to identify federal government PKI requirements; recommend policies, procedures, and standards; provide oversight of PKI activities in pilot projects; and make recommendations regarding establishment, demonstration, and operation of a federal PKI. However, the council's plans do not include the formulation of specific plans for PKI implementation throughout the government nor does the strategic plan set as an objective to develop a management framework document that would integrate and codify guidance on PKI development.

Conclusions

The federal government must overcome a number of substantial challenges before PKI technology can be widely and effectively deployed. These challenges include providing interoperability among agency PKIs, ensuring PKI implementations can support a potential large scale of users, reducing the cost of building PKI systems, setting policies to maintain trust levels among agencies, and establishing training programs for users at all levels. Although such challenges are difficult to overcome in the near term, the federal government can take steps to better assist agencies at developing and implementing PKIs that may eventually be interconnected into a federal governmentwide system. The recent effort to develop a FBCA is an excellent first step in this direction, but this activity currently lacks the context of a well-defined program plan for the government as well as key policy and technical standards. Establishing a federal PKI management framework could facilitate and accelerate participation in the FBCA as well as overall federal adoption of a key technology for enabling electronic government.

Recommendations for Executive Action

Although federal agencies are accountable for assessing their own information security risks and determining what measures they will take in response, OMB has statutory responsibility to develop and oversee policies, principles, standards, and guidelines used by agencies for ensuring the security of federal information and systems. As such, we recommend that the Director, OMB:

- Establish a governmentwide framework to provide agencies with direction for implementing PKIs. Recognizing the government's evolving efforts in implementing PKI technology, OMB's framework should encompass initiatives currently being developed by the CIO Council, such as the activities of the FPKISC and the FBCA, as well as existing guidance related to PKI issued by NIST and the Department of Justice.

To construct this framework, we further recommend that the Director, OMB, take the following specific steps:

- Develop federal PKI policy guidance in order to (1) facilitate the use of PKI, (2) ensure that agency PKI applications meet consistent levels of security, and (3) reduce the overall risk to the government of developing disparate PKI implementations. The guidance should discuss the full range of policy issues relevant to PKI—including privacy, trust levels, encryption key recovery, and long-term proof of identity and authenticity.
- Ensure the development and periodic review of technical guidance, such as high-level APIs, as use of PKI technology in the public and private sectors broadens and standards develop and mature.
- Ensure the preparation of a program plan for the federal PKI, including implementation of the FBCA. The program plan should define roles and responsibilities among participating agencies and identify milestones and resources needed to develop, deploy, and maintain a federal PKI and associated applications, including the need for PKI-related training.

- Ensure, through ongoing oversight of federal information security activities, that agencies are adhering to federal PKI policy and technical guidance, including providing justification for nonparticipation in the FBCA.

In implementing these recommendations, OMB should work with other key federal organizations, especially the CIO Council, FPKISC, and NIST, to ensure broad acceptance within the federal government.

Agency Comments and Our Evaluation

We received comments on a draft of this report from OMB, GSA, DOD, the Chairman of the FPKISC, and Treasury. All of the agency officials who reviewed the draft agreed with the overall content of the report. However, comments and discussions with officials from OMB and GSA raised concerns about the intent of our draft recommendations. Specifically, the OMB and GSA officials were concerned that the recommendations language in our draft report would lead OMB to adopt an overly prescriptive "how to" role in federal PKI implementation. In response to OMB and GSA concerns, we have clarified the language outlining our recommendations to focus on OMB's role in establishing a governmentwide PKI framework that recognizes the government's evolving efforts and encompasses initiatives that are currently underway. We have also clarified the major elements that should be included in this framework—policy and technical guidance, a federal PKI program plan, and oversight.

In commenting on our draft recommendations, GSA expressed concern about potential adoption of a "one size fits all" approach to PKI technical solutions, architecture, and policy. GSA stated that it endorses a broad range of solutions to meet individual agency electronic business needs. We believe that a comprehensive management framework—as we have defined it in the report and clarified it in our recommendations language—would provide a consistent and disciplined approach to assist agencies in examining alternatives, making risk-based decisions, and determining appropriate levels of security for their PKIs and associated applications. The framework would not assume or replace the program and security responsibilities of individual federal agencies but would, rather, help them meet the objectives of a federal PKI and reduce risk for the government as a whole. For example, the framework would include policies, standards, and technical guidance providing for a range of implementation approaches that agencies can choose from to satisfy their individual requirements. At the same time, adherence to the framework would promote interoperability and help reduce costs by guiding agencies away from developing unique and noninteroperable PKIs.

Regarding our discussion of the value of a federal PKI architecture, GSA commented that, in its opinion, the ACES program already serves this role. We disagree. The ACES program is too narrowly focused to serve as a model architecture for the entire government. ACES is aimed at facilitating transactions with the public (as opposed to interagency and intra-agency applications) and offers services on a contractual basis to agencies that choose not to develop their own internal PKI infrastructure. In addition, agencies are not required to use ACES in developing their PKIs, nor has the technical architecture of ACES been designated a model for the federal government. Therefore, however useful it may be for certain purposes, ACES does not serve as a governmentwide PKI architecture. In addition, as noted elsewhere in the report, DOD has stated that the binding between an individual and their public key is not secure enough to meet their needs.

DOD, the FPKISC Chair, and Treasury commented on the challenge of affordability discussed in our report. While the agencies all agreed with our discussion of the high cost associated with implementing PKI technology, they commented that the long-term benefits of assured electronic communications should justify the expense. We believe the report, taken as a whole, provides a balanced picture of the need for PKI, coupled with the cost challenge that the government faces in implementing it. However, we have made revisions to our discussion on affordability—particularly start-up funding—to clarify this point.

DOD concurred with the report, stating that the recommendations for executive action all appeared to be prudent for successful implementation of a PKI across the federal government. In regard to our recommendation for a comprehensive management framework, DOD stated that our recommendation should "quantify" the continued roles of the FPKISC and CIO Council within the framework. Although it is OMB's responsibility to define the precise roles of these and all other nonstatutory entities within the federal PKI management framework, we agree that the FPKISC and CIO Council should continue to play important roles in the development of PKI in the federal government, and have revised our recommendations to clarify this point.

Treasury commented that the draft report accurately captured technical and policy efforts to date and offered a series of editorial and clarifying comments. OMB also offered a series of clarifying comments. These have been addressed as appropriate throughout the report.

Limitations of the Secure Sockets Layer Protocol

A common method of facilitating secure connections through the Internet is to use a protocol known as the secure sockets layer (SSL) to encrypt data that are transmitted between a user's computer and the server supporting an electronic commerce Web site. This technology uses a limited form of PKI to provide confidentiality for the transaction. Commonly available Web browsers (such as Microsoft's Internet Explorer and America Online's Netscape Communicator) have built-in software that uses the SSL protocol to obtain digital certificate information that can be used to authenticate the server that they are connecting with and establish an encrypted session between the user and the server, based on public key cryptographic techniques. This process provides confidentiality for customer information such as the customer's name, address, and credit card information.

Although SSL can provide confidentiality during a transaction and perhaps some degree of authentication, as commonly configured and used it does not provide other important security services. For example:

- Unless the user manually checks and has a way to personally validate the certificate presented by the Web-based server during the SSL process, there is no real assurance of the identity of that server (authentication). Furthermore, manual review of the certificate is not a simple process. Users may have to navigate several menu selections to find certificate information and determine if the name on the certificate is the same as that of the site they believe they are visiting. Second, they need to consult the authority that issued the certificate to determine if the certificate has been revoked, i.e., whether it can still be trusted. Third, they need to review the process that was used to bind the server to that certificate and determine whether that process is adequately secure. This is because some certificates are issued using very weak processes that offer little real assurance. For example, some certificates can be obtained simply by contacting one of the certification authorities that issue these kinds of certificates and paying a fee. Such a process does not provide assurance that the server is operated by the entity named on the certificate.
- Although data traveling between the server and the user are encrypted, once such data are received and stored locally by the server, the data may not be encrypted. For example, recently a major financial services company was successfully attacked and unencrypted customer credit card numbers were obtained (violating confidentiality). Additionally, a successful attack against a server storing unencrypted data could allow an attacker to compromise the data in a manner that might not be detected (violating data integrity).

- Although a more recent version of the SSL protocol allows the server to authenticate the user, in order for this process to work, the user must have a digital certificate. However, many users do not have these certificates. In addition, just as with the server certificates, no effective process is in place to validate a user's identity before issuing a certificate (violating authentication).
- Although it is used for electronic commerce transactions, SSL does not provide all the needed assurances for these transactions. Credit card laws and policies compensate for security weaknesses and significantly contribute to confidence in the system, since credit card owners can repudiate bogus transactions. It is up to the merchant to prove that the customer did in fact make the transaction (issue of nonrepudiation).

Certification Path Models for Building Large PKIs

For the full benefits of PKI technology to be realized, there must be a way to combine separate systems into larger connected networks of trust, such as a single large federal PKI, which could in turn be subsumed within a larger national or international network. To do this, each component within the larger network of PKIs needs a way to reliably recognize and trust digital certificates generated by the other components. Three conceptual models have been proposed for achieving this objective: (1) reliance on trust lists embedded in Web browsers, (2) having certification authorities organized into a single hierarchy, and (3) organizing certification authorities as a mesh. Each model has strengths and weaknesses, and a clearly superior method has yet to emerge.

Trust Lists

The first approach to trusting digital certificates issued externally to a specific PKI involves using predetermined "trust lists" of external certification authorities. (See figure 9.) Using this approach, a file containing self-signed certificates for each trusted certification authority is placed in each user's Web browser. The user's computer will accept a certificate only if it is directly signed by one of the listed certification authorities. Users can control the file and add to or remove certification authorities from the list.

Figure 9: Trust List Certification Path

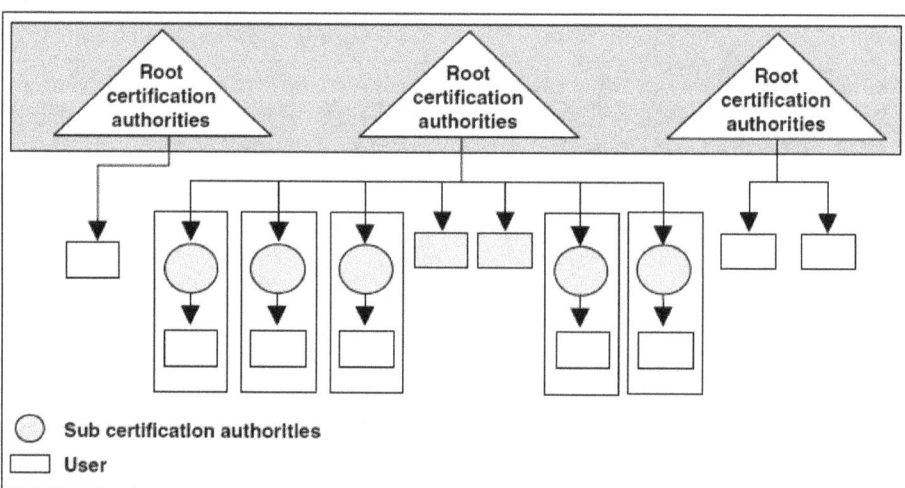

Source: Federal Public Key Infrastructure Steering Committee.

This model is currently the most widely used, as software to support it is built into the two most popular browsers on the market.[1] It is relatively simple, straightforward, and easy to implement. It allows the individual user to have complete control over which certification authorities he or she trusts. The simple certification path may also speed processing.

Despite its widespread use, this approach has several drawbacks that result in weak security assurances. First, the inclusion of a default list of certification authorities in the prepackaged browser software provides no way to ensure that the list is accurate. In fact, the list will have to be constantly updated in order to reflect the addition or deletion of certification authorities. As a result, no means exists to check for prompt certification revocation. Second, the fact that the end user controls the list of certification authorities creates an opportunity for users to subvert an organization's assurance objectives. For example, a user may decide to accept invalid digital certificates inserted by a hacker or signed by a certification authority that the organization or agency has not approved. To prevent such problems, the organization needs to continually determine, update, and maintain—on each user's computer—its official list of trusted certification authorities, as well as indications of the trust levels associated with the certificates issued by those certification authorities, and how those certification authorities are to be identified as trusted in agency application software. As a result, the management of this potentially large list may be too difficult and time-consuming for most organizations.

Hierarchical Model

In order to support a more systematic and ordered method for checking digital certificates, a hierarchy of certification authorities is sometimes used. (See figure 10.) The basis for this model is the designation of a single "root" certification authority that is trusted by all users. The root certification authority issues certificates to subordinate certification authorities, which may in turn issue certificates to even lower-level certification authorities. This hierarchy may be many certification authorities deep. Because each authority's certificate is signed by a higher authority, the user can always verify the validity of a particular certificate by tracing the certification path back to the known and trusted root.

---

[1]The software included with these browsers relies on the secure sockets layer (SSL) protocol. Limitations of SSL are discussed in appendix I.

Figure 10: Hierarchical Model Certification Path

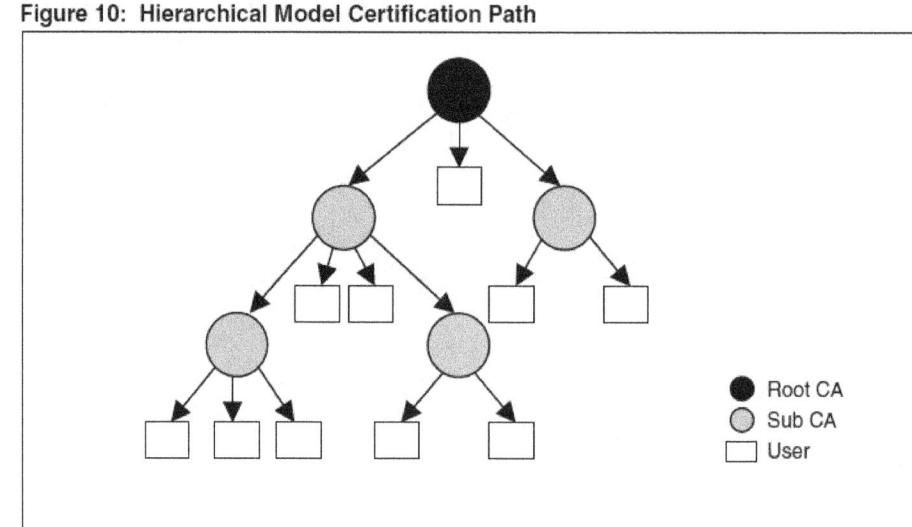

Source: Federal Public Key Infrastructure Steering Committee.

This model has both advantages and disadvantages. First among its strengths is that the process to validate users' certificates is straightforward, as each user has a certification path back to the root certification authority. Simplifying the certificate validation makes it easier for one organizational unit to accept certificates created by another. This hierarchical model also lends itself to the management structure of many organizations, such as agencies of the federal government.

A drawback to this approach is that the root certification authority represents a single point of failure; if it is compromised, all subordinate certification authorities and all certificates that have been issued are compromised and will have to be replaced. Additionally, since many federal agency PKIs are likely to be independently developed and funded, it is unlikely that agreement could be reached on a single root PKI for the entire federal government. Finally, the potential for very long trust paths can have a negative impact on processing efficiency.

Mesh Architecture

A third approach is to establish nonhierarchical links among certification authorities that are not subordinated to each other. This is known as a mesh or network architecture. (See figure 11.) Independent certification authorities cross-certify one another and issue each other certificates. The resulting electronic credentials are known as "cross-certificate pairs," and are the basis for a mesh of trust relationships between certification authorities. A recipient of a digital certificate may not have a direct trust relationship with the certification authority that originated the certificate for a given transaction. But the recipient's PKI software can determine whether that certificate is to be trusted by starting with the one or more certification authorities that are already established as trusted and determining whether a chain of cross-certificate pairs can be followed back to the originating certification authority.

Figure 11: Mesh Architecture Certification Path

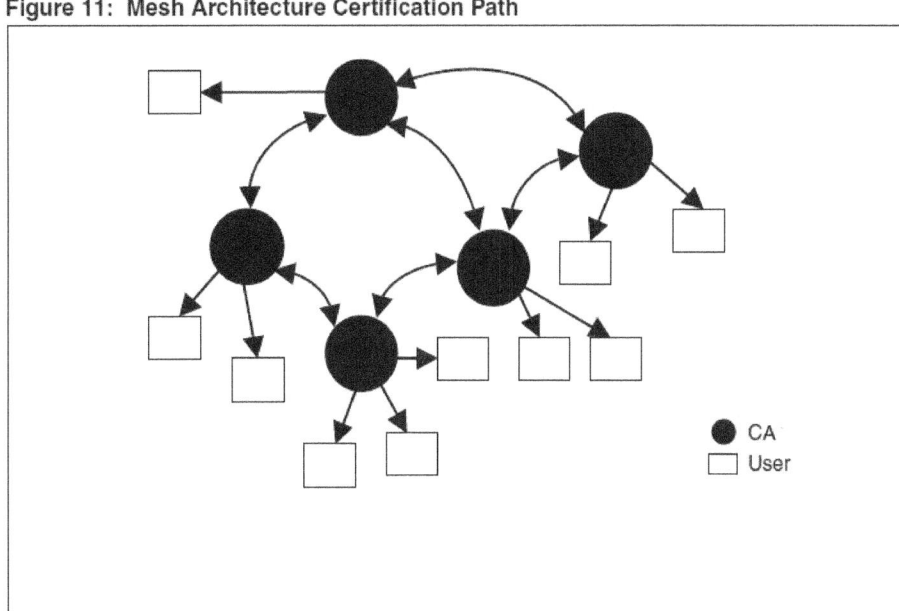

Source: Federal Public Key Infrastructure Steering Committee.

This peer-to-peer model has distinct advantages. It is flexible, facilitating ad hoc associations and trust relationships, and reflects the bilateral trust of transacting parties. It allows the direct cross-certification of certification authorities whose users communicate frequently, which reduces the amount of processing time necessary to generate the certification path. And if one of the certification authorities is compromised, the negative effect on the rest of the network is minimized. Certificates would have to be reissued for only that one certification authority and its users. Drawbacks to this model include the fact that finding a valid certification path can be complex and can consume a lot of computer processing time. A user cannot provide a single certification path that is guaranteed to enable verification of his or her certificates by all other users.

Comments From the Department of the Treasury

DEPARTMENT OF THE TREASURY
WASHINGTON, D.C. 20220

JAN 19 2001

Mr. Joel C. Willemssen
Managing Director
Information Technology Issues
United States General Accounting Office
441 G Street N.W., Room 4T31
Washington, DC 20548

Dear Mr. Willemssen:

The Chief Information Office has reviewed the draft report entitled Information Security: Advances and Remaining Challenges to Adoption of Public Key Infrastructure Technology Integrity and submits the attached comments.

We appreciate the opportunity to review the draft report and commend GAO on the comprehensive review. The report accurately captures our technical and policy efforts to date. We suggest some minor editorial modifications for completeness and clarity; these are contained in the enclosure.

If you require additional information, we will be happy to assist. Please contact Kim Phalen of my liaison staff on 202-622-3255 with any issues.

Sincerely,

James J. Flyzik
Deputy Assistant Secretary (Information Systems)
and Chief Information Officer

Enclosure

Comments From the General Services Administration

GSA Office of Governmentwide Policy

January 17, 2001

Mr. Joel C. Willemssen
Managing Director, Information Technology Issues
U.S. General Accounting Office
441 G Street, NW.
Washington, DC 20405

Dear Mr. Willemssen:

The Office of Governmentwide Policy appreciates the opportunity to review and comment on the Draft Report GAO-01-277, Information Security: Advances and Remaining Challenges to Adoption of Public Key Infrastructure.

The Governmentwide Policy agrees with the two basic premises of the report that:

- Public Key Infrastructure (PKI) is critical technology to provide electronic government services and the Government has made progress in planning and coordinating the implementation of PKI across the Federal Government; and,

- Full, interoperable PKI implementation across Government is complex and presents many challenges.

The Governmentwide Policy agrees that substantial progress has been made, but there is much that still must be accomplished in order to support widespread, interoperable PKI services across Government. In this regard, we do not believe there can be a "one size fits all" approach to PKI technical solutions, architecture, or policy. Rather, we endorse implementation of a broad range of solutions to meet individual agency e-business needs. The Federal Bridge Certificate Authority and the Access Certificates for Electronic Services (ACES) program lay the foundation for widespread, interoperable PKI trust networks throughout the Federal Government. We will continue our commitment to work in cooperation

U.S. General Services Administration
1800 F Street, NW
Washington, DC 20405-0002
www.gsa.gov

- 2 -

with Federal agencies, committees, and industry to build the technological infrastructure to support the needs for secure government e-business. We welcome the opportunity to work with your office to accomplish this.

The enclosure provides our comments to the Draft Report. Per your request, our comments include those of the current Federal PKI Steering Committee Chair. Our comments consists of three sections:

- Section 1: Comments on each of the four recommendations for executive action presented in the Draft Report.

- Section 2: Specific comments from Judy Spencer, Chair of the Federal PKI Steering Committee.

- Section 3: Technical comments on the report text.

Again, we appreciate the opportunity to offer these comments. If you would like to discuss these comments in more detail please contact John Sindelar at 202-501-8880 or Judy Spencer at 202-708-5600.

Sincerely,

G. Martin Wagner
Associate Administrator
Office of Governmentwide Policy

Enclosures

1) GSA comments on the Draft Report Information Security: Advances and Remaining Challenges to Adoption of Public Key Infrastructure

Federal Recycling Program   Printed on Recycled Paper

Glossary

Agency CA	An agency CA is a certification authority that acts on behalf of an agency and is under its operational control.
Application Programming Interface	The application programming interface is the interface between the application software and the application platform (i.e., operating system), across which all services are provided.
Authentication	Authentication is a security measure designed to establish the validity of a transmission, message, or originator, or means of verifying an individual's authorization to receive specific categories of information.
Backup	Backup copies of files and programs are made to facilitate recovery if necessary.
Binding	Binding is the process of associating two related elements of information.
Certificate	A certificate is a digital representation of information that at least (1) identifies the certification authority issuing it, (2) names or identifies the person, process, or equipment that is the user of the certificate, (3) contains the user's public key, (4) identifies its operational period, and (5) is digitally signed by the certification authority issuing it. A certificate is the means by which a user is linked—"bound"—to a public key.
Certification Authority (CA)	A CA is an authority trusted by one or more users to issue and manage X.509 public key certificates and certificate revocation lists.
Certification Path	Certification path is a method used by PKIs for recognizing and trusting digital certificates issued by other PKIs in order to create larger, connected networks of trust. Three conceptual models for creating certification paths include (1) trust lists, (2) hierarchical model, and (3) mesh architecture.

Certificate Policy	Certificate policy is a specialized form of administrative policy that addresses all aspects of the generation, production, distribution, accounting, compromise recovery, and administration of digital certificates. By controlling critical elements of a certificate's data structure, a certificate policy and its associated enforcement technology can support provision of the security assurances required by particular applications.
Certification Practice Statement	A certification practice statement is a statement of the practices that a CA employs in issuing, suspending, revoking, and renewing certificates and providing access to them, in accordance with specific requirements (i.e., requirements specified in the certificate policy or requirements specified in a contract for services).
Certificate Revocation List	A certificate revocation list is a list maintained by a CA of the certificates it has issued that have been revoked prior to their stated expiration date.
Compromise	Compromise is the disclosure of information to unauthorized persons, or a violation of the security policy of a system in which unauthorized intentional or unintentional disclosure, modification, destruction, or loss of an object may have occurred.
Confidentiality	Confidentiality is the assurance that information is not disclosed to unauthorized entities or processes.
Cross-Certificate	A cross-certificate is a certificate used to establish a trust relationship between two certification authorities.
Data Integrity	Data integrity is the assurance that data are unchanged from creation to reception.
Digital Signature	Digital signature is the result of a transformation of a message by means of a cryptographic system using keys such that a relying party can determine (1) whether the transformation was created using the private key that corresponds to the public key in the signer's digital certificate and

	(2) whether the message has been altered since the transformation was made.
Electronic Government	Electronic government involves the use of network technology (especially the Internet) to provide on-line public access to government information and services and to improve internal business operations.
Encryption Certificate	An encryption certificate is a certificate containing a public key that is used to encrypt electronic messages, files, documents, or data transmissions, or to establish or exchange a session key for these same purposes.
Federal Bridge Certification Authority (FBCA)	FBCA is a system of certification authorities, directories, certificate policies, and certification practice statements designed to provide peer-to-peer interoperability among federal agency principal certification authorities.
Federal Public Key Infrastructure Policy Authority	This authority is a federal government body responsible for administering and enforcing policies regarding how agency PKIs will interoperate through the FBCA.
Government Paperwork Elimination Act	This act, Public Law 105-277 (October 21, 1998), sets a deadline of October 21, 2003, for agencies of the federal government to develop capabilities to permit, where practicable, electronic maintenance, submission, or disclosure of information, including the use of electronic signatures.
Hierarchical Certification Path Model	The hierarchical model is a conceptual model for creating a certification path that is based on the designation of a single "root" certification authority trusted by all users. The root certification authority issues certificates to subordinate certification authorities that may in turn issue certificates to lower-level certification authorities.
Integrity	Integrity is the assurance that data are protected against unauthorized modification or destruction of information.

Interoperability	Interoperability is the ability of two or more systems or components to exchange information and to use the information that has been exchanged.
Key Pair	A key pair includes two mathematically related keys that have the following properties: (1) one key can be used to encrypt a message that can only be decrypted using the other key and (2) even knowing one key, it is computationally infeasible to discover the other key.
Mesh Certification Path Model	The mesh model is a conceptual model for creating a certification path that establishes links among peer certification authorities.
Nonrepudiation	Nonrepudiation is the assurance that the sender is provided with proof of delivery and that the recipient is provided with proof of the sender's identity so that neither can later deny having processed the data. Technical nonrepudiation refers to the assurance a relying party has that if a public key is used to validate a digital signature, that signature had to have been made by the corresponding private signature key. Legal nonrepudiation refers to how well possession or control of the private signature key can be established.
Peer CA	Peer CA is a CA in a mesh certification path that has a self-signed certificate that is distributed to its certificate-holders and that is used by them to start certification paths. Peer CAs are not subordinated to other certification authorities; instead, they cross-certify one another.
Principal CA	The principal CA is a CA designated by an agency to interoperate with the FBCA. An agency may designate multiple principal CAs to interoperate with the FBCA.
Privacy	Privacy defines restricting access to subscriber or relying party information in accordance with federal law and agency policy.

Private Key	The private key is (1) the key of a signature key pair used to create a digital signature, or (2) the key of an encryption key pair used to decrypt confidential information. In both cases, this key must be kept secret.
Public Key	The public key is (1) the key of a signature key pair used to validate a digital signature or (2) the key of an encryption key pair used to encrypt confidential information. In both cases, this key is made publicly available, normally in the form of a digital certificate.
Public Key Infrastructure (PKI)	PKI is a system of hardware, software, policies, and people that, when fully and properly implemented, can provide a suite of information security assurances—including confidentiality, data integrity, authentication, and nonrepudiation—that are important in protecting sensitive communications and transactions.
Registration Authority	Registration Authority belongs to an entity responsible for identification and authentication of certificate subjects, but not for signing or issuing certificates (i.e., a registration authority is delegated certain tasks on behalf of an authorized CA).
Relying Party	The relying party is a person or agency receiving information that includes a certificate and a digital signature verifiable with reference to a public key listed in the certificate, and in a position to rely on them.
Revoke a Certificate	To revoke a certificate means to prematurely end the operational period of a certificate effective at a specific date and time.
Risk	Risk is the expectation of loss expressed as the probability that a particular threat will exploit a particular vulnerability with a particular harmful result.
Root CA	In a hierarchical PKI, the root CA is the CA whose public key serves as the most trusted datum (i.e., the beginning of trust paths) for a security domain.

Server	A server is a system entity that provides a service in response to requests from clients.
Signature Certificate	A signature certificate contains a public key intended for verifying digital signatures rather than for encrypting data or performing any other cryptographic functions.
Subordinate CA	In a hierarchical PKI, the subordinate CA is a CA whose certificate signature key is certified by another CA and whose activities are constrained by that other CA.
Threat	A threat is any circumstance or event with the potential to cause harm to an information system in the form of destruction, disclosure, adverse modification of data, and/or denial of service.
Tool Kit	In the context of PKI, a tool kit is a suite of software used to develop or modify applications so that they effectively perform encryption, decryption, digital signature generation, or other cryptographic operations. Most commercial tool kits are based on proprietary data interfaces that work only with one vendor's products.
Trust List	A trust list is a conceptual model for creating a certification path that is based on a standardized collection of trusted certificates used by relying parties to authenticate other certificates.
X.509	X.509 is the most widely used standard for defining the format for digital certificates.

Sources: Federal Public Key Infrastructure Steering Committee; Institute of Electrical and Electronics Engineers, Inc.; National Security Telecommunications and Information Systems Security Committee.

Related GAO Products

Bank Regulators' Evaluation of Electronic Signature Systems (GAO-01-129R, November 8, 2000).

Internet Privacy: Federal Agency Use of Cookies (GAO-01-147R, October 20, 2000).

The Challenge of Data Sharing: Results of a GAO-Sponsored Symposium on Benefit and Loan Programs (GAO-01-67, October 20, 2000).

Electronic Government: Opportunities and Challenges Facing the FirstGov Web Gateway (GAO-01-87T, October 2, 2000).

Financial Management Service: Significant Weaknesses in Computer Controls (GAO/AIMD-00-305, September 26, 2000).

Electronic Government: Government Paperwork Elimination Act Presents Challenges for Agencies (GAO/AIMD-00-282, September 15, 2000).

Information Security: Serious and Widespread Weaknesses Persist at Federal Agencies (GAO/AIMD-00-295, September 6, 2000).

Internet Privacy: Agencies' Efforts to Implement OMB's Privacy Policy (GAO/GGD-00-191, September 5, 2000).

Defense Management: Electronic Commerce Implementation Strategy Can Be Improved (GAO/NSIAD-00-108, July 18, 2000).

Electronic Signature: Sanction of the Department of State's System (GAO/AIMD-00-227R, July 10, 2000).

Information Security: Fundamental Weaknesses Place EPA Data and Operations at Risk (GAO/AIMD-00-215, July 6, 2000).

Information Security: Vulnerabilities in DOE's Systems for Unclassified Civilian Research (GAO/AIMD-00-140, June 9, 2000).

Electronic Government: Federal Initiatives Are Evolving Rapidly But They Face Significant Challenges (GAO/T-AIMD/GGD-00-179, May 22, 2000).

Federal Information Security: Actions Needed to Address Widespread Weaknesses (GAO/T-AIMD-00-135, March 29, 2000).

Information Security: Comments on Proposed Government Information Security Act of 1999 (GAO/T-AIMD-00-107, March 2, 2000).

Information Security: Weaknesses at 22 Agencies (GAO/AIMD-00-32R, November 10, 1999).

Critical Infrastructure Protection: Fundamental Improvements Needed to Assure Security of Federal Operations (GAO/T-AIMD-00-7, October 6, 1999).

Information Security: Many NASA Mission-Critical Systems Face Serious Risks (GAO/AIMD-99-47, May 20, 1999).

Indian Trust Funds: Interior Lacks Assurance That Trust Improvement Plan Will Be Effective (GAO/AIMD-99-53, April 28, 1999).

Information Security: Serious Weaknesses Place Critical Federal Operations and Assets at Risk (GAO/AIMD-98-92, September 23, 1998).

Customs Service Modernization: Architecture Must Be Complete and Enforced to Effectively Build and Maintain Systems (GAO/AIMD-98-70, May 5, 1998).

Identity Fraud: Information on Prevalence, Cost, and Internet Impact Is Limited (GAO/GGD-98-100BR, May 1, 1998).

Tax Systems Modernization: Blueprint Is a Good Start But Not Yet Sufficiently Complete to Build or Acquire Systems (GAO/AIMD/GGD-98-54, February 24, 1998).

Social Security Administration: Internet Access to Personal Earnings and Benefits Information (GAO/T-AIMD/HEHS-97-123, May 6, 1997).

Air Traffic Control: Complete and Enforced Architecture Needed for FAA Systems Modernization (GAO/AIMD-97-30, February 3, 1997).

Corps of Engineers Electronic Signature System (GAO/AIMD-97-18R, November 19, 1996).

Information Superhighway: An Overview of Technology Challenges (GAO/AIMD-95-23, January 23, 1995).

Ordering Information

The first copy of each GAO report is free. Additional copies of reports are $2 each. A check or money order should be made out to the Superintendent of Documents. VISA and MasterCard credit cards are accepted, also.

Orders for 100 or more copies to be mailed to a single address are discounted 25 percent.

Orders by mail:
U.S. General Accounting Office
P.O. Box 37050
Washington, DC 20013

Orders by visiting:
Room 1100
700 4th St. NW (corner of 4th and G Sts. NW)
U.S. General Accounting Office
Washington, DC

Orders by phone:
(202) 512-6000
fax: (202) 512-6061
TDD (202) 512-2537

Each day, GAO issues a list of newly available reports and testimony. To receive facsimile copies of the daily list or any list from the past 30 days, please call (202) 512-6000 using a touchtone phone. A recorded menu will provide information on how to obtain these lists.

Orders by Internet:
For information on how to access GAO reports on the Internet, send an e-mail message with "info" in the body to:

info@www.gao.gov

or visit GAO's World Wide Web home page at:

http://www.gao.gov

To Report Fraud, Waste, or Abuse in Federal Programs

Contact one:

- Web site: http://www.gao.gov/fraudnet/fraudnet.htm
- e-mail: fraudnet@gao.gov
- 1-800-424-5454 (automated answering system)